ERNEST MANGNALL

THE ARCHITECT OF MANCUNIAN FOOTBALL

GW00481905

IAIN McCARTNEY

EMPIRE
PUBLICATIONS

EMPIRE PUBLICATIONS

1 Newton Street, Manchester M1 1HW

© Iain McCartney 2022

ISBN: 978-1-909360-99-0

Contents

INTRODUCTION

I HAVE BEEN SUBMERGED in the history of Manchester United Football Club for more years than I care to remember. The players, the games, the ground. Anything in fact related to the club, be it the past under the guise of Newton Heath or the modern day United. A mirror image it certainly is not.

Through numerous books and countless articles, I couldn't estimate how many words I have written relating to the club and, having recently formed the 'Manchester United Graves Society', many of those players who once pulled on the shirt have become much more than a name to me as I have traced their burial (or cremation place) and looked at their career and background a little more closely than before. Snippets of some careers were already known; others took a bit of research.

There was, however, one individual whose grave was found not to be in the best of condition. The stone cross that had previously stood on top of a plinth had somehow fallen onto the grave and had lain like that for some considerable time. However thanks to a United Supporters organisation, Stretford Enders Worldwide, money had been donated to the Graves Society to be used if and when required. Here now was the ideal opportunity to put those funds to good use, as this was not simply any grave, it was that of James Ernest Mangnall, manager of the club between September 1903 and August 1912. Not only was he the first proper manager of the newly-formed Manchester United but he was the first to win a trophy for the club, guiding the Reds to the First Division championship in 1907-08 and the FA Cup the following year before adding a second title in 1910-11.

Enquiries regarding the possibility of having the grave restored to its former glory were made and the local Lytham St Annes authorities were only too happy to allow the work to take place. The project quickly took shape. A United supporting Manchester-based stone mason was approached, a figure quoted and the go ahead given. Unfortunately, no-one saw the approach and disruption that Covid-19 would cause, but as summer 2020 blended into autumn, the work was carried out and the grave restored.

I was more than happy to have played a part in that story, but as boredom continued, despite the dreaded virus at long last showing signs of easing, I needed something to pass the time. I had already penned two books over the past months and both sat with publishers, ready to be printed and hit the shelves, but I needed yet another project to pass the time.

After contemplating numerous possibilities, one night the name Mangnall flashed through my mind, for no particular reason. The seed was planted, some rough form of research was done and the decision made. The story of James Ernest Mangnall had to be told.

Hopefully you find it as enjoyable to read as I did to write.

The inspiration for this book came following the discovery and restoration of Ernest's grave as detailed in the Introduction, through my work with the Manchester United Graves Society, which restores and documents the final resting places of former players, managers and administrators.

1: A TALE OF TWO MANGNALLS

JAMES ERNEST MANGNALL was born in the Belmont area of Bolton to Joseph and Ann (nee Hart) Mangnall on May 30th 1864, the couple's third child, although some sources give the date of birth as January 4th 1866, which is incorrect. A brother, John Edward Mangnall, had been born two years previously, his sister Jane Annie Bell Mangnall, twelve months before, but she had unfortunately died the same day as she was born. 1866 saw the birth of another brother, Joseph Montell Mangnall, but again the family were struck by bereavement as he was to die a mere three years later. Another sister, Augusta Anne was born in 1867 and thankfully she was to enjoy a much longer life than her two siblings.

Trying to lay the foundations of Mangnall's career in football is a difficult task, as it is with any player from the 1800's, but it is documented that he was an inside forward whilst playing with Bolton Grammar School and Bolton Grammar School Old Boys and later a goalkeeper in his youth, going on to win representative honours for Lancashire. So, burning the midnight oil and delving through countless newspapers, the name J. Mangnall does indeed appear as goalkeeper for Eagley, a club formed around 1874 and one of the first clubs to play the game under the Association rules and also one of the founder members of the Lancashire Football Association in 1878.

Three years after that formation we stumble across J. Mangnall not simply playing for the Eagley club but captaining them, as a half-back against Westhoughton in a 4-0 victory. It was a victory that most probably brought nothing more than local bragging rights, or even 'one-upmanship' on a workmate, but the six-year-old Eagley club were possibly a notch or two above some of their neighbours as they were able to field not simply one team come Saturday afternoon, but three, as occurred in February 1878 when their first XI, albeit with only nine men, faced a twelve-man team called 'Commission Street' and won 4-0. A second eleven faced St James and won 7-0, while the third team came up against the St James 2nd team and won 6-0. Not a bad afternoon's work.

But wait a minute, 1878? That would make our subject a mere fourteen years old, (twelve if you take the 1866 date as his birth year) raising the question, were there two J. Mangnall's playing the game in the same area at this particular time? It is a question with no real answer, as initials rather than names are more commonly used and even with our Mangnall being J. E., only one is used and it was not until later in life that he was to become known as Ernest rather than James. To throw further fuel on the fire, there was also a John Mangnall from Eagley playing the game who was also involved with the Lancashire F. A. This involvement, however, appears not to be in a playing capacity, but as the Association's auditor.

If you want your proof documented in good old black and white, let's look no further than a small article in the *Cricket and Football Field* newspaper of July 9th 1910 – "In his more youthful days Mr. Mangnall played both Association and Rugby with Bolton Grammar School, and with sundry other clubs".

There is nothing to say that a fourteen-year-old could not be playing for Eagley at this time, as they were indeed formative years of the game and if you had the ability and were around the club, or the area where they played, then there is every possibility that you would get a game.

Eagley must have been a bit more than just a 'capable' side, as even against stronger sides they managed to hold their own, as on Saturday February 9th 1878, Mangnall and his players come up against the might of Darwen and held them to a creditable 2-2 draw.

Apparently, something of an all-round individual, the Eagley team of November 1878 that faced Sheffield Albion at their ground near to Bromley Cross at Turton shows Mangnall, again as captain, in the forward line. The change of position was not to bring victory, as the Sheffield side, reputed to contain "some of the finest Association players in the north of England", ran out winners by two goals to nil.

Perhaps they were able to field three teams, but when faced with stronger opposition, Eagley often struggled, finding themselves more often than not on the defensive, as they were a couple of weeks prior to that fixture against the Sheffield side, as Blackburn Rovers beat them by a similar score line. But on other Saturday afternoon's Mangnall and his team mates could match the best, even when obstacles were put in their way, as happened on November 30th 1878 when they came face to face with Bolton Wanderers at Pike's Lane.

Arriving at the Wanderer's ground with only nine men, they had to call on the services of two spectators, one of whom was a Bolton Rovers player, but they still managed to record a 2-0 victory and even allowed their hosts to call on a substitute when one of their players were injured.

A matter of months after facing Turton as an inside-forward, we find J. Mangnall between the sticks against the same team in the Turton Challenge Cup Final at Chapleton, the home of Eagley's opponents, where around 2,000 witnessed an exciting encounter, which Eagley won by a solitary goal.

Some might be of the opinion that the visitors should have registered a few more as Haworth, the Turton centre-forward was off the field injured for the entire second half, but it was not simply a deserved victory, but also a moral one, as Turton had commandeered one or two individuals from Darwin to assist them that afternoon, much to the disapproval of some of those lining the ropes. One of those 'guest' players was the famed Fergus Souter, who is reckoned to be the first professional footballer in the English game. Souter was also to appear as a team-mate when the duo were selected to play for Lancashire a short while later.

Also in the opposition was J. J. Bentley, a name that would become linked with Mangnall in later years and a player who it was written about "played for Turton in his early teens", perhaps revealing the answer that Mangnall did indeed play for Eagley at an early age.

Something that conjures up the impression that there could well be two J. Mangnall's comes to light on January 2nd 1879 when Partick Thistle ventured south to face Blackburn Rovers at the East Lancashire Cricket Club at Alexandra Meadows when we find J. Mangnall involved, not in the playing side of the game, but as referee. Is this the same man, or could it be the auditor, or even someone completely different?

Sometime in between November 1878 and February 1879 Mangnall was transformed from a forward to a goalkeeper, as J. Mangnall appears as Eagley's goalkeeper against Astley Bridge on January 11th 1879. Nothing is mentioned as to why such a change took place, but quite probably it was due to the regular custodian being injured or not turning up, as was normally the case when such a position change occurred but he must have taken to the position well, perhaps due to his involvement with rugby, as he was selected to represent the recently formed Lancashire Football Association against North Wales at Wrexham in February 1879.

His involvement in the 2-1 victory must have been creditable, as were his performances in the weeks and months that followed, as he played further games for the county side against Staffordshire and North Wales again later that year. September 1879 also saw him line up for Turton and Eagley to face Bolton and District. This fixture was to see him praised for *"the manner in which he defeated their charge"*.

Having seen the outfield Mangnall being named as Eagley's captain, the re-incarnation of Mangnall the goalkeeper is now captain of the Eagley side and a regular feature in their line-ups against local opposition such as Lower Chapel Edgeworth, Bolton Wanderers, Accrington and rivals Turton, and against opposition from slightly further afield such as Stoke and Sheffield Albion.

Mangnall was also the Eagley goalkeeper when they made their first venture into the F.A. Cup, where they came up against the might of Darwen, a team that contained a Glaswegian by the name of Fergus Souter, who ventured south from Partick Thistle to the Lancashire side and who is considered to be the first professional footballer. Having been given a bye in round one, Eagley travelled to Darwen on December 7th 1878 and on a bone hard pitch, due to overnight frost, the conditions, considered "totally unfit for play", proved to be the master of both teams and the score line remained blank. Despite the strength of the opposition, Eagley had held their Darwen counterparts to draws the previous season, but in the replay, fourteen days later, again played amid atrocious conditions with the pitch covered in three inches of snow, and witnessed by some 3,000 brave souls, Darwen progressed into the next round on the back of a 4-1 victory.

For this game goalkeeper Mangnall is listed as captain, but there is already a question mark beside the name – is it really 'our' James Ernest as this would make him, as previously mentioned, only fourteen years old while Souter, on the other hand, was twenty-one, and would a mere teenager be given the captaincy?

But how young in fact was he, if indeed this 'Mangnall' is our 'J. E.', because if we fast forward for a moment to 1906, he was married in July of that year and his age is given as thirty-six, meaning he was born in 1870, adding further confusion to the situation.

As you have read, a J. Mangnall officiated the match between Blackburn Rovers and Partick Thistle on January 2nd 1879, so it might come as something of a surprise that on New Year's Day 1880 we also see him playing as a 'guest' for Turton against Partick Thistle, with the *Bolton Evening News* correspondent at the match writing: *"Mangnall on several occasions averting a score for Partick."* Avert goals he may have done but he also conceded a handful in the 5-3 defeat.

Mangnall also receives a mention in a report of a game against Sheffield Albion in February 1879 which mentions that he was responsible for one of the visitor's five goals, catching the ball in his arms, but allowing it to slip through his legs.

But his outfield days were certainly not behind him, as during a fixture against Lower Chapel at Knowle Heights, Darwen, in a Lancashire Association cup-tie in January 1880, with his team losing 5-1 at half time, he relinquished his position as the last line of defence and took over at centre-forward. It was of little avail as Lower Chapel scored three more to Eagley's one.

Football was a far different game back in those distant days, not simply in the rules, style of play and attire, even the line-ups would seem strange to modern eyes as they would list a goalkeeper, two backs, two half-backs and six forwards. A simple glance at a match from that period would probably be like watching a kick-about in the park: there was no penalty area as we know it today, the addition of a crossbar or 'tape' had just been introduced (previously a goal could be scored by booting the ball at any height between the posts as in modern day Aussie rules), goal nets were still two decades away while the game was officiated by two on-field umpires and it wasn't until 1881 that a referee was introduced to adjudicate in disputes. Pitches were not of a uniform shape and there was no law governing either the length of the match or the number of players per side until 1897. It was against this background that Mangnall continued to thrive and in the often sparse reports he can be found "staying away many stinging shots" and generally giving a good account of himself.

In an article which appeared in the *Sporting Chronicle* of Wednesday December 10th 1879, and headed "The Association Game In Lancashire", Eagley are described as being "a very hard-working eleven, and with a little more polish would render a good account of themselves in any company", adding "Mangnall at goal is wonderfully clever at times". By 1881, however, the name of Mangnall is missing from the Eagley line-up either as a goalkeeper or outfield player, but it does appear with much regularity as either an 'umpire' or referee and continues to do so for the next year or so, but it wasn't without its problems.

On Saturday 11th March 1882 he officiated the Bolton Wanderers v Darwen fixture at the Trotters' Pike's Lane ground. As Bolton had never defeated their opponents, there was much interest in the game and despite the rather unfavourable weather over 2,000 were present. The afternoon did not get off to the best of starts, as play didn't commence until 3.45, but once that game got underway, the majority of the action was centred around the Darwen goal. But then, with twenty minutes played, the visitors broke away and scored. The Wanderers, shaken by this goal scored against the run of play, immediately appealed for offside and Mr Brownlow of Bolton Olympic, who was referee, was in agreement with those appeals and disallowed the goal. Play was soon back at the Darwen goal and following a scrimmage with a Bolton player clearly in an offside position, the ball found its way between the posts. Darwen were loud in their appeal for offside, but on this occasion the referee allowed the goal to stand.

Darwen were understandably upset at losing a goal in such circumstances and they considered the referee to be totally against them and asked for him to be removed from the game and when he wouldn't agree to step down, the Darwen players walked off. Placed in an awkward position the home side agreed to the referee's removal and Mangnall came on in his place. Thankfully, the remainder of the afternoon passed without further controversy and the game ended in a 2-2 draw.

The name of Mangnall continues appear with some regularity in the early years of the 1880's as an umpire or a referee, but in the latter half of that decade it is difficult to trace his whereabouts until November 1889 when he once again surfaces in a peace-keeping role, as a steward at the Bolton Cyclist Ball, a joyous affair by all accounts, with dancing and 'refreshments' until 3.30am!

But his young life, never mind his sporting career, might well have come to a premature end in April 1881. His father, having previously seen employment as a joiner, was now recorded in the 1881 Census as being a 'Beer Seller' at his home at 45, Coe Street, Bolton, where health and safety appears to have been somewhat low in the priorities, as the *Bolton Evening News* of Wednesday April 13th reported:

> "*ACCIDENT IN A BREWERY. An elevated boiler in the brew house of Mr. Joseph Mangnall, of 45, Coe-street, fell about quarter past six o'clock on Tuesday night. A son Mr. Mangnall was slightly injured about the head and leg, and the brewing apparatus was considerably damaged.*"

Ernest then found his life turned upside down in 1882 when his mother died and his father re-married four years later. It is open to debate as to whether or not the teenager got on with, or even approved of the marriage, but in 1891, he was found to be in lodgings with an Albert List and his family in Lostock, near Bolton, whilst working as a machine fitter. It is perhaps an interesting 'add-on' that Albert List was a coachman and groom to the Lever family whose son, William, went on to be co-founder of Lever Brothers and who would later become first Viscount Leverhulme. For how long James Ernest was employed as a machine fitter is anyone's guess, but it could have been no more than a source of income, as his mind was always on sporting activities. Now in his mid-twenties cycling appears to be Ernest's passion as March 1890 finds a Mr J. E. Mangnall of 11 Nelson Street, Bolton holding the position of Honorary Secretary of the Bolton Cyclist Club and it is from this point that we can begin to paint a more definitive picture of his life.

Cycling was a growing leisure pursuit for people of all classes with clubs cropping up all over the industrial north as increased leisure time allowed enthusiasts to pedal along the deserted country lanes of rural Lancashire to escape the smog and filth of the urban landscape and get a bit of fresh air. Yet for Ernest Mangnall riding a bike wasn't simply a nice day out, he remained a sportsman and was a little more enthusiastic as regards the competitive side of the sport.

June 1890 finds him at the Bolton Church Institute Athletic Sports event, held on the grounds of Bolton Cricket Club. Among the twenty-two events on the programme was the one-mile bicycle handicap, in which he was one of five entrants and one of only two who started from scratch. Reports of the race relate that:

> *"The runners had not gone far before Mangnall came a cropper, knocking Berger down. The latter remounted and though he had lost ground he pulled up well at the finish."*

A member of the Bolton Harriers club, there were numerous opportunities for racing and more relaxing rides and the sport appears to be one that was widely enjoyed and highly competitive. There are mentions of the Harriers taking on the Highfield Harriers with a run to Wigan, with Mangnall finishing second. It wasn't, however, all up hill and down dale, as cross-country events were also a regular feature on the cycling calendar.

His term as secretary of the Bolton Cycle Club came to something of an abrupt end at the club's AGM of January 1892, when: *"The club's indefatigable secretary was rejected from that office by a narrow majority"*. The report of the meeting in the *Cricket and Football Field* went on to say:

> *"It was hard lines, but the old ordinary rider says he will be glad of a little rest. During his three years service as secretary J.E.M. has been unremitting in his exertions and unsparing in his use of midnight oil, and it is mainly to this that the B.C.C. has attained the proud position it now enjoys."*

With cycling being such a prominent sport of the time, it received good coverage in the newspapers of the day and in the likes of Mangnall had its personalities, with individuals who could pedal faster than others finding the bicycles of the day a form of equipment that they could easily adjust to.

The sport also had its followers, as a letter to the *Cricket and Football Field* of March 12th 1892 revealed.

> *"I have received the following communication from a correspondent anent the selection of the Bolton Harriers' team for the Junior Championship: - 'Dear Velox, - On reading your cross-country notes on Saturday, I was much struck by the absence of a very familiar name among the Bolton Harriers' selected team for the Northern Junior C.C. Championship. Of course, I refer to the genial J. E. Mangnall. Now to my mind, I think a thoroughly*

representative cross-country team incomplete without him, as also is a local cyclist club, for that matter, as I have no doubt the B.C.C. will find to their cost this season. Last year I, along with him, ran in the Championship race for the honour of B.H., and although he did not figure in the front rank it was not for the want of pluck, as all his club mates can testify. Why he not amongst the chosen ten this year I am at a loss to understand. Yours Truly, Anglezanke.'"

Like all sporting equipment of the period, bicycles were far removed from those of today and back in 1892 Mangnall rode a "Buckingham and Adams light pneumatic roadster". Those bicycles could have either pneumatic, solid or cushion tyres and were priced at between £8 and £16. I doubt very much if there was any form of sponsorship at that time, but Mangnall and the above mentioned bike appear in print together on a number of occasions with the likes of, *"J.E. Mangnall ran third in the two miles at the* [Bolton] *Institute Sports on his new Buckingham and Adams' roadster"* finding its way into the notes about the sport.

Swimming and boxing could also be found on his Ernest's CV, something that is confirmed in his testimonial programme from 1924, but trying to trace his involvement in the latter two sports is like searching for a needle in a haystack. The best I can do is locating a J. Mangnall playing rugby for Heaton [who may have played at the football club ground at Great Lever] around 1883, whilst on the swimming front there was a J. Mangnall prominent in the Tyldesley Swimming Galas of 1887 and 1888, winning £1 for coming first in the six-length handicap, and £2. 10/- for again coming first in a handicap race, having given the field a thirteen second start and finishing a yard in front of the champion. This 'Mangnall' is recorded as being a 'fine swimmer' and a 'future captain of the Tyldesley Swimming Club'. But as before, the question is again asked – is this our Ernest?

Away from the sporting arena he also took an interest in politics as he is mentioned in July 1892 as working hard on behalf of the two vice-presidents of the Bolton Cycling Club in the Parliamentary elections. He could also be considered something of an entertainer as a 'hot-pot' evening for the Cycle Club was brought to a close by T.E. Lee, J. E. Mangnall, A. Hargreaves, Mears and Bateson.

Mangnall thrived on his involvement within a sporting environment and is listed as Honorary Secretary for an 'Old English Sports and Gala' event at Halliwell in April 1893, while he was seeking a band for their Annual Sports Day in September of that same year. Not only had he moved from one club to another, he was now residing at 136 Kestor Street in the town.

By now, perhaps Mangnall's days in the saddle in a competitive nature were past, as he was now twenty-nine and had ridden from Bolton to John O'Groats, a total of some 510 miles, in five days and 17 hours. It is also reported that he also went in the opposite direction – Bolton to Land's End, but no time has been recorded. So, stepping back from road and cross-country racing, and retaining his involvement at a representative level, he took his involvement that one step further by opening a cycle shop in Nelson Square, Bolton.

In regards to the Land's End to John O'Groats exploit, it was regarded as "*a feat which becomes something like an adventurous journey when the details are told by J.E.M. The physical endurance of the man and the appalling weather at times, nearly makes one wonder that he survived the ordeal."*

Life must certainly have been far from dull, as he had also been a keen cross-country runner and was Honorary Treasurer of Bolton Harriers, while continuing to be Honorary Secretary of the 'Bolton Cyclist Club'. He was also a life member of Farnworth Cycling Club and the district representative of the National Cyclist's Union in Bolton.

By this point in his life football had seemingly been long forgotten, although it is more than likely that a Saturday afternoon would have found him among friends watching one of the local sides but August 1895 saw his interest in the game re-kindled. Bolton Wanderers had begun life as a Sunday School club known as Christ Church back in 1874, changing its name in 1877 following a difference of opinion with the vicar. Their ground at Pike's Lane was far from ideal; a heavily muddied pitch, situated at the foot of a hill, it nevertheless attracted decent crowds, with one report from an FA Cup replay against Notts County mentioning that there were between 4,000 and 5,000 enjoying the game, with an enterprising farmer charging half the price of admission of the club by to allow them to watch from a vantage point in his field. Losing money was far from ideal and coupled with an increase in rent from £83 to £175 over the course of a dozen years, and with local builders keenly eyeing the site, a decision was made to move on.

A five-acre plot owned by the Gas Committee was found on Manchester Road and a fourteen-year lease was agreed at an annual rent of £130, but the Burden Park site was far from ideal, with a railway line on one side and a refuse and chemical dump on the other but it would be Wanderer's home for most of the next century.

Burnden Park was officially opened on Saturday August 17th 1895 with a gala sports day and J. E. Mangnall was involved as the clerk of the course. Within three years he was back again in an official capacity, but this time, far removed from ensuring that an afternoon's sport event ran smoothly he was now a director of the club, a big step up from simply being on the 'Ground and Sports Committee', but he took the appointment in his stride and during his time on the board he never missed a game home or away. Initially he had become involved due to his enthusiasm in sport and he joined the committee whose responsibilities were to oversee the construction of a cycling and running track, while it had also been his aim, his dream, to see an athletic ground built in the town.

Being a Bolton Wanderers director did little to dilute his love affair with the bicycle and at times the two wheels may well have overtaken the round ball, with his interest far from confined to Lancashire, as October 1896 saw him cross Hadrian's Wall and head for Glasgow to organise the 'Glasgow Cycle Show', something he co-promoted with a Mr Foster. Such was its success that the city's St Andrew's Halls hosted a second 'Cycle Show' in March 1897.

The financial side of football back in those formative years was, to many, a constant thorn in the side and Bolton Wanderers were no different than countless other clubs up and down the country. As Mangnall was a director and the name that stood as a guarantee at the local bank, he had on occasion to put his hand in his pocket, which often made the difference between the players being paid or not. How deep his pockets were I have no idea, but he was to write: *"I was, along with others, a guarantor at the bank, and I found wages for the players when we had no other source to obtain them from than our private purses. I was very enthusiastic over the game and I never missed a meeting or a match. There is a common saying which is tagged on to sport, and which in my case can be applied to football. It is that if business interferes with football, then the business must be dropped. In my case I pretty nearly did it. I was at the beck and call of the club for everything, and I was not a wealthy man. What I could possibly stand for I did."*

As well as financial assistance, Mangnall and his fellow directors were also to give the club physical assistance, removing their jackets, rolling up their sleeves and deputising for horses to ensure that the Burnden Park playing surface was in tip-top condition. If cutting the grass saved the club money, then Mangnall would do it without a murmur.

But J. E. Mangnall's involvement in an official capacity with the Wanderers almost came to an end on the evening of May 31st 1899, when he was amongst "a very good attendance" at the AGM of Bolton Wanderers Football and Athletic Co., which was perhaps something of a solemn occasion, due to the club having been relegated to the Second Division at the end of the season that had recently drawn to a close.

According to the 'Articles of the Association', six directors were due to retire, but the whole body of the directorate, thirteen in total, including Mangnall, decided to offer themselves up for re-election. It was then agreed that the board would be reduced to eight. He had his supporters within the ranks, as he was re-elected with 165 votes, the fifth highest.

By the end of the year he had taken a further step up the ladder but not with Bolton Wanderers, as Christmas Day 1899 saw him appointed secretary/manager of

Lancashire rivals Burnley, a position for which he had been overlooked for a year or two previously at Bolton.

From a list of between seventy and eighty applicants, he was offered the position *"at the somewhat dubiously fabulous salary of £156 per annum."*

2: TRYING TIMES AT TURF MOOR

BURNLEY WERE A RELATIVELY young club compared to Bolton, having been formed in May 1882, but had strode into the world of professional football the following year and if J. E. Mangnall enjoyed a challenge, which I think he clearly did going by his sporting heritage, then Burnley was an ideal place for him. Moving from a Second Division club to one in the First would also have had its plus points.

Burnley had been without a secretary for a few months following the departure of Mr. H. Bradshaw to Woolwich Arsenal, with a couple of committee members taking over the reins in the interim, hence the results in the first half of the 1899-1900 season being something of a mixture having played seventeen games, winning five, drawing four, but having lost eight. Crowds hovered between 5,000 and, on a good day, almost 13,000, when local opposition such as Blackburn Rovers were in town.

The new man at the helm came under the spotlight in the *Lancashire Evening Post* on Monday March 12th when a lengthy profile appeared beginning:

> *"No better man could have been selected, and so far, everything has gone to prove that Mr. Mangnall is well qualified to undertake the onerous duties. Recognising his wide experience in matter appertaining to football and athletics the directors have endowed him with full powers and are placing no obstacle in his way in managing the team and the club."*

It proceeded to mention that whilst on the Bolton directorate he:

> *"Was the man chosen as best fitted to take sole charge of the players, and, apart from that, he practically had sole charge of the team as far as training was concerned for two years".*

Adding his accomplishments in the cycling world in holding numerous records for 'the solid tyre' in the Bolton area.

> *"These facts all prove that Mr. Mangnall has been through the mill. Of course, he does not care to enter into a critical analysis of the capabilities or otherwise of the Burnley players, but he makes no secret of the fact that he regards Hillman as having no superior goalkeeper. Training has naturally been a special study with the Burnley secretary, but he knows that a lot depends upon the men themselves, if they are to be fit for their work. No matter, he says, what special training is given a player, and care taken of him, if he does not look after himself when training is done for the day, the labour is really thrown away. It is not good, he considers, to give the men too much practice with the ball. Some people seemed to think players should have the ball every day but once a week was plenty in his estimation. On Saturday they had hard work, and was not advisable to stiffen their muscles by continual kicking, but on the other hand, make them more pliable by moderate exercise. Fully recognising the varied degrees of physical endurance possessed by players, he pointed out that the great aim in training a team should be to keep*

the men in a fairly good condition throughout the whole season. If they were required to be fit for a special match it was easy to get them in the pink of condition, but when a player had to stand the whole season consideration ought to made for that fact. There was as much harm done by over-training as under-training. Mr. Mangnall has also his own views with regard to the treatment players. He believes in handling them as men, and finds he can get more work out of them by such a policy, accompanied with tact, than otherwise. So far as the Burnley players are concerned, these measures have certainly been productive of goodwill and a clear and full understanding between both parties. There is not shadow of doubt that Mr. Mangnall has started the right track in Burnley, and both the chub and players will benefit by his experience. He may have ambitions in many directions, but his chief one certainly is to build in Burnley a team which will be the envy of footballdom."

That Mangnall enjoyed a challenge cannot be disputed as he was to relate as regards his new appointment:

"Burnley was in very low water at the time I joined the management. They were in the First Division, it is true, but there was held very strongly in certain directions that owing to our strained financial resources we might the better profit if we fell out of the premier division into the Second. Naturally, the expenses entailed by a club in the lower division are considerably less than those associated with a club in the First Division. I saw the possibility of the club being better able to meet its liabilities by an

economic drive, but I was against the idea of falling into the second on principle. We had a good set of men, capable of putting up a good game of football, and I was a believer in making the game popular with the public by giving them the very best that could be provided, even if we had to scrape the money. However, despite my hopes and ambitions, at the end of the season we found ourselves actually beaten into the Second Division."

A 2-2 draw against Nottingham Forest, two days prior to Mangnall's appointment had left the Clarets just below mid-table in eleventh place on fourteen points. They were a long way off leaders Sheffield United (who had 31 points) and only four points above bottom club Preston North End. Mangnall's first game in charge was against Stoke City on Boxing Day and it was far from the best of starts in his new environment, suffering a 3-0 defeat in the Potteries. Four days later in his first home match in charge, he managed to rally his troops and an Edgar Wallace Chadwick hat-trick was enough to take the two points against Glossop North End in a 3-1 win.

Victory, however, proved to be something of a rare occurrence, as Ernest was to find his first managerial appointment far from rosy. Defeats continued to out-number victories, with goals being a major problem as the campaign moved towards a close. In the second half of the season inconsistency reigned supreme. Burnley would lose one, then win one, a sequence that lasted for six games and had it continued then there is every possibility that the Turf Moor side would not have found themselves in the relegation zone.

A 3-0 victory over Notts County on March 3rd

saw them still occupying eleventh place. Glossop were bottom, eight points worse off, while near neighbours Blackburn Rovers were one place and two points above the North End club. Then the wheels really came off with only one victory in the next seven games. That solitary victory came against Liverpool on April 7th, a 1-0 away win bringing a surprise two points by all accounts and a result that should have seen a corner turned and First Division survival kick-started, as it left Burnley third from bottom, three points above second bottom Preston North End and level on points with Blackburn Rovers and Liverpool.

Mangnall, however, could not maintain the positive momentum. An away fixture at Wolverhampton Wanderers the following Saturday produced a 3-0 reversal, which was followed seven days later with a relegation battle against Preston North End at Turf Moor. It was a fixture that attracted much attention, with around 9,000 present and a victory for the home side would have assured top flight football for another season at least. Burnley had their chances, which they refused to take and when Preston scored the only goal of the match, much in the way of debate ensued as the players and officials of the home side argued for offside against a Preston forward. The referee ignoring their pleas.

So two games remained and it was to be either Mangnall's side or Preston North End for the drop with a solitary point separating the clubs. Preston held an advantage as their two remaining fixtures were pencilled in for April 28th – Wolverhampton Wanderers and April 30th - Blackburn Rovers, with both games at Deepdale. Burnley on the other hand faced Sheffield United at Turf Moor on April 23rd and Nottingham Forest at Trent

Bridge on April 28th.

Burnley took a step towards safety with a solitary goal victory against Sheffield United, but it was back to that single point on the 28th, as two Forest goals in each half left Mangnall and Burnley's First Division hopes hanging by a thread, as Preston defeated Wolves 2-0 that same afternoon.

Only one First Division fixture of the 1899–1900 season remained to be played and that saw Blackburn Rovers making the short trip across Lancashire to Preston. A defeat for the North End side would see their great rivals Burnley relegated, while a draw would be enough to save the Clarets as they had a superior goal average. In the event Rovers failed to save their near neighbours, something that may well have been more profitable to do, and showed little in the way of enthusiasm, conceding two without reply, thus condemning Burnley to the Second Division.

Mangnall did not intend for Burnley's involvement in Second Division football to extend beyond one solitary season and he was soon on the search for individuals to improve the team. Not only that he felt that it would be beneficial to the club if he spent more time in an administrative role, leaving the training to others, although he would continue to oversee such matters in the long term, hence the advert in the local press:

> *"Two Efficient Trainers for first and second teams respectively, - Apply, stating age, experience and salary required, to J. E. Mangnall, 25 St James's Row, Burnley."*

Hopes of a brief sojourn in the Second Division of the Football League were frustrated by a third place finish in their first season back in the lower league. In mid–April 1901, with two games remaining, they were third, two points behind Small Heath who had played two games fewer and four points behind leaders Grimsby Town. Those two games, against Stockport County away and promotion rivals Small Heath at home, were crucial. As it turned out the Stockport fixture was lost and so was the chance of promotion as Small Heath, despite defeats in one of their games in hand and also at Burnley on that final day of the season, claimed the runners–up spot.

In regards to that final ninety minutes against Small Heath, an *Athletic News* correspondent wrote:

> *"There were not many over 1,000 people present at Turf Moor to see the fall of the curtain in the football drama – some folks would describe it as a tragedy. Of course, the only interest centred in the question as to whether Burnley would, as three years ago, preserve an unbeaten home record. This they did, so that compared with 1897-98 they have only lost one point. If the team had done as well on foreign soil the club would now be in the First Division."*

Why Mangnall's men found it so difficult away from home remained something of a mystery. On their own patch, points and goals went hand in hand. They scored five in consecutive fixtures against Glossop North End and Chesterfield, four against Blackpool and Barnsley and an unmatched seven against a hapless Newton Heath in the FA Cup.

Home, they say, is where the heart is or, in Burnley's case, was certainly where the results were, but in March 1901 Mangnall wondered if the townsfolk had the club in their heart, as a lack of finance was proving as much of an opponent as the eleven men facing his team on a Saturday afternoon. Preston North End were offering their players £100 if they could avoid relegation from the First Division. If Burnley's Second Division rivals Grimsby Town were to achieve promotion, then the locals were going to get behind them with a special fund, while Small Heath's financial success had propelled them to within touching distance of the First Division. Not one to miss an opportunity, Mangnall attempted to secure financial assistance from those within the locality.

Not only were those within Burnley likely targets for a Mangnall fund–raising spree, he occasionally cast his eyes further afield. When he joined the club it was considered that £25 was an exceptionally good gate, but when the opportunity to make £15 for more or less nothing, by allowing the ground to be used by a third party, Mangnall jumped at the chance...

> "*I thought I had done a good stroke of business for the club when I arranged with a menagerie for £15 for them to make the ground their pitch during the show's stay in Burnley, and drew up an agreement with the advance agent. The show came along at 4 a.m., but the elephants could not get through the slush and get the waggons in. After pulling the place to pieces, they left it and went on to the Market Place. I went round at night and saw the boss who refused to pay. I told him I had got an agreement and that if I did not get my money, I would have his performance stopped the next day. 'Well,' he said, 'you can't have it now, except in threepenny bits and copper.' 'I do not care if I have it in halfpennies', I replied and he paid me in*

copper and I carted it away."

His attempts to raise the financial and footballing profile of Burnley did not go unnoticed out with the town, nor did his own personal ambition. In October 1901 a vacancy arose for the position of secretary of Everton due to the retirement of the current holder of the post, a Mr Molyneux, a former Liverpool coal merchant, and Mangnall threw his hat into the ring. A correspondent with the much respected, and widely read *Athletic News* reacted thus: *"I have known Mr. Mangnall personally for a good number of years and if the Everton people care to take my word for it, they need have no better man. He has unlimited power at Burnley, but what can a man do with a club that is £3,000 behind?"* The writer continued: *"In his application, he is supported by testimonials from three Lancashire members of the League Committee, Messrs Bentley, Lewis and Sutcliffe, who should know how he conducts his business."*

The vacancy itself conjured up considerable interest, with 128 applications with the £300 salary perhaps the main attraction. This was whittled down to seven – Mr Cuff, who was an Everton director and already acting as interim secretary; Mr W. Wallace of Dundee; Mr Thomas Maley of Celtic; Mr Wilson, secretary of the Liverpool and District Football Association, Mr Dickie Boyle, an international half-back, Mr Wales of the *Liverpool Mercury* and J. E. Mangnall. This was reduced further after the initial interviews, with Mangnall failing to make the cut, the position going to the man who already had his feet under the table.

Dejected by his failure to make the final short list and indeed obtain the position itself, Mangnall got on with the job at hand with Burnley, but it was turning out to be something of a thankless task, with the financial side of things continuing to prove troublesome. The AGM of June 1901 saw Mangnall report that owing to the miserable support accorded the club in the previous season *"they were compelled to part with several good players"*. Such matters must have been unsettling and they certainly were not going away anytime soon, as a year down the line it came to light that Burnley were *"just managing to pay their way"*. Season 1901-02 saw the Clarets fall well short of challenging for a promotion place, finishing in mid-table, twenty-one points behind second placed Middlesbrough and a further four behind champions West Bromwich Albion. Two points fewer and an inferior goal average would have seen them in the mix of applicants seeking re-election.

From challenging for promotion to the top flight to suddenly hanging on by your fingertips to Football League status in a matter of two years, it must have been a tremendous blow to Mangnall and the people of Burnley. This was the position that the club found itself in by the end of the 1902-03 season.

As per normal, their home form was passable, if not exactly brilliant, winning half a dozen and drawing seven of their seventeen fixtures. Away from Turf Moor, however, their form was abysmal, losing sixteen of the seventeen fixtures and drawing the other. It was of little surprise that they finished bottom. There was, however, no instant relegation, as only two divisions existed, but the bottom three clubs had to apply for re-election, along with, on this occasion, five other applicants.

At the annual meeting of the Football League at the Tavistock Hotel in London's Covent Garden on Monday May 25th, Burnley had a nervous wait as there were more pressing matters than the Lancashire club's fate. It was even more nail biting when the outcome as to what three clubs would be participating in the Second Division the following season was announced. Newly formed Bradford City secured thirty votes, Stockport County, who had finished second bottom, received twenty, leaving Burnley in something of precarious position, as Doncaster Rovers, the other Second Division side who were applying for re-election had finished third bottom. It was either going to be one or the other and the voting fell in favour of Burnley by nineteen to fourteen.

Having to apply for re-election must have been embarrassing for Mangnall, adding to the frustration of having to part with the services of his best players. He was a man who wanted the best in whatever field he found himself in, but at the same time he was realistic in knowing that he could only work with what he had and money was as scarce as points. Indeed, there was many a time during his Burnley tenure that he did not draw a salary as the money was simply not available.

Although money was scarce, he could always scrape together enough to purchase the odd player, but despite his persuasive powers, he didn't always get his man. One of those failures was Jimmy Quinn, a notable Scottish player who was with Smithton Albion at the time and went on to become one of the greatest centre-forwards north of the border with Celtic. Having somehow heard about Quinn, Mangnall headed north and found him still in his pit clothes. *"A very nice spoken man"* recalled Quinn, *"but I had some job getting rid of him. He had a lot of nice things to say about the town of Burnley and tried to convince me that I would make a fortune there, if I would just sign. He offered me £2.10s a week and £10 bonus if I signed. He said I would be one of the highest paid players in the team."*

When asked what his reply was, he said he wasn't going and when asked why, he said that he had already signed for Celtic, even although he had yet to play a game for them. Despite trying to get Quinn to change his mind, Mangnall on this occasion was unsuccessful, but was to return on at least another two occasions to try and get his signature.

He prepared for the 1903-04 season in his usual fashion, relieved that his team were still a league club, while he was also to be seen as forward thinking when it came to attempts to top up the club's piggy-bank, as an advert in the *Burnley Express* of Saturday September 26th 1903 shows – *"Burnley Football Club. Tenders invited for the sole right of selling all kinds of refreshments on the ground during season 1903-04. Caterer to have the option to sub-letting. Advertisements wanted for the Stands, etc. Tenders to be sent to J. E. Mangnall, Turf Moor, on or before Thursday, October 1st."*

In comparison to recent seasons, the 1903-04 campaign got off to a favourable start, with six points from the opening quartet of fixtures. A point at Chesterfield as the season got underway was followed by a 2-0 victory against Manchester United, a 0-0 draw against local rivals Bolton Wanderers and a solitary goal victory over Port Vale, all three fixtures at Turf Moor. The first reversal didn't come until September 26th, 2-0 against Preston North End at Deepdale. Determined to do the best for the club was still at the forefront of Mangnall's mind, but he knew that his days at Turf Moor were drawing to a close, as four days after the defeat by table topping Preston, he joined Manchester United following the resignation of James West. Strangely, the same day that the *Manchester Evening News* reported that Mangnall was joining United (September 30th), the advert regarding the selling of refreshments and advertising once again appeared in the *Burnley Express* with the Tenders still to be sent to Mangnall at Turf Moor!

The move south came as something of a surprise to many of Mangnall's friends as they were aware that he had turned down numerous offers of employment elsewhere in recent times, always rejecting those advances as he was disinclined to leave Burnley while in such a difficult position. There was, however, no animosity nor annoyance as regards his decision to walk away from the club, with the departure reluctantly accepted.

An article in the *Lancashire Evening Post* on Friday October 2nd read:

> *Thanks to his hard work on behalf of the club, the prospects are now fairly bright, and when the offer of the United secretaryship was made to him by Mr. J. J. Bentley, Mr. Mangnall felt himself justified in severing his connection with Burnley, his own directors, whilst sorry to lose him, advising him to take the course he has done his own interests.*
>
> *When Mr. Mangnall came to Burnley the club was in low water, but by careful attention to all the details of management, he has placed the organisation once more on a sound footing. To show the true position of affairs during his tenure office, a few figures are necessary. In 1899-1900 the wage bill amounted to £3,282, the match receipts were £3.277, and the loss on the season's working was £706. In 1900-1 the figures were: - Wages. £2.349; receipts, £1.926; loss. £806. In this year, it will be remembered, Burnley made a big struggle to regain entrance into the First Division*

In 1901-2 the wages had decreased to £1546, and the receipts £1,252, and the loss, be it carefully noted, was only £4 16s. 2d. Last season there was a further shrinkage of wages (£1.019), and receipts (£946) but the loss had risen to £61. An interesting comparison with the total receipts last season (which included all matches. Belvedere, cup ties, &c.) and the receipts of three league matches this season may here be made in the reader's mind, for these latter engagements have brought in no less than £370!

The figures given clearly indicate that the outlook is now much brighter than ever it has been during Mr. Mangnall's career at Turf Moor. He himself holds that the fortunes of the club were never so rosy, for the finances are now in order, - and the club has an excellent team at command. Mr. Mangnall will take up his new duties next week and will leave Burnley with the best wishes of the many friends he has made by his kindly, genial disposition."

Mangnall's departure from Turf Moor was not simply a case of emptying his desk drawers, saying goodbye to the players and staff and walking out the door into the sunlight. It was much more than that and showed just what sort of a man he really was. On the evening of Wednesday October 14th he entertained the Burnley directors and players to dinner at Cronkshaw's Hotel, a noted establishment in the town. After everyone had been fed and watered Mangnall referred to:

"The loyal and friendly way in which he had been treated by everyone connected with the club, which

> *had passed through a very trying time during the*
> *past three seasons. He was glad to say they seemed*
> *to have at last turned the corner, and he hoped the*
> *club would have a prosperous career in the future.*
> *He asked the players to act towards his successor,*
> *Mr. Whittaker, as they had acted towards him."*

He added that he would be pleased to do his best for Burnley, always, of course, after Manchester United.

In proposing a toast to the health and continued success of the former manager, the chairman of the club (Councillor Whitehead) said:

> *"Burnley Football Club was losing a true and*
> *valued servant. No one knew more than Mr.*
> *Mangnall the troublous times the club had passed*
> *through, and there was hardly another football*
> *secretary in England or Scotland that would have*
> *done what Mr. Mangnall had for Burnley."*

He went on to say that he hoped those Burnley experiences *"would never be repeated, for he had had a very severe training in football management."*

Following on from the chairman, Mr. C. E. Sutcliffe, a director, said *"he had been brought very closely into touch with Mr. Mangnall. and they had both known something of the downs of football."* He went on to recall one of the most miserable journeys they had ever had together, when they travelled to London at the end of the previous season, more or less cap in hand, seeking re-election to the Second Division. Sutcliffe went on to say that *"there was not a club in the history of football that had had so much bad luck as Burnley, but he believed they had now turned the long lane."* Referring to Mr. Mangnall, Sutcliffe said that he was going to one of the few clubs that had immense resources.

As for Mangnall himself, he was later to say:

> *"Although no man had ever more difficulties to contend with and hard work in connection with the game, I feel bound to state that those days I spent at Burnley were the happiest ones of my life. If we won, we won, and if we lost, we lost. There were no recriminations any more than there was insincere praises. There was never an unkind word passed between the management and myself; never a word in fact, that reflected anything but satisfaction and the highest comradeship and fraternity. I do not plead ignorance to the fact that at one period Burnley was referred to by supporters of other teams as 'Dirty Burnley'. But in recalling this today, allowances must be made for the period, and I am not so sure now with all the weight at weight in the akin to gladiatorial combats of those stirring days, that the game was not cleaner than it is today from the view point of real injurious fouls."*

Burnley had not simply lost their man at the helm, but an individual who had done everything possible in his attempts to make the Turf Moor side more than capable of jousting with the best in the country. In four years he had only spent £10 as a transfer fee, buying James Lyndsay, a player he was later to sell to Bury for £200. He was also to obtain £300 from Manchester City for Jack Hillman. He even went four months without a salary himself and could also be found cutting the grass to save on expenses. Nothing was beyond him, nor discouraged him, not even the regular difficulty of arranging a committee meeting as the members were always of the opinion that their secretary would, at some point, ask for money. They were often more wrong than right.

8		9	10	11	12
Name and Surname of each Person		**RELATION to Head of Family**	**Condition as to Marriage**	**Age last Birthday of**	
				Males	Females
Frank A. Rist		Son		12	
James E. Mangnall		Visitor	S	34	
James Taylor		Head	M	52	
Mary	do.	wife	M		27

An extract from the 1901 census which places thirty-four year-old Ernest Mangnall as a 'visitor' at 135 Kenton Street, Bolton where he is listed as Secretary of Burnley FC.

First row:—J. E. Mangnall (Secretary), Councillor E. Whitehead (Chairman).
Second row:—J. Stuttard (Trainer), Ross, Barron, Taylor, Lockhart (Captain), Howarth, Tawler, Dixon, O. Pickles (Groundsman).
Third row:—Hegan, McInnes, Crawford, Lea.
BURNLEY.
Photographed by J. S. Wilkinson, Manchester.

Mangnall (left, back row) in his role as Burnley Secretary. Ernest's time at Turf Moor was a struggle. A lack of money meant he was always dreaming up ambitious money-making schemes.

3: MANGNALL UNITED

MANCHESTER UNITED may well have had "immense resource" in the eyes of Charles Sutcliffe, but that hadn't always been the case. Formed back in 1878 by workers of the Carriage and Wagon works at the Newton Heath depot of the Lancashire and Yorkshire Railway, it had simply been an additional form of recreation, after a hard day's toil, an addition to the cricket team, keeping some of the workforce at least out of the local public houses for a couple of hours. Having a football club was also beneficial as a means of attracting workers if they also had an interest in the round ball game, whilst, as it matured, being used as a form of incentive, offering employment within the industry to footballers of ability.

Keeping members of the team out of public houses was a difficult task, as Heath's ground at North Road had no changing rooms, so the players changed at the Three Crowns public house and trotted down the road along with their supporters to play their fixtures.

Those early fixtures were little more than friendlies, taking on a more competitive edge in 1889 when admission to the Football Alliance was gained, kicking off with a 4-1 victory over Sunderland Albion. But with victories came defeats, both on and off the field, as attempts to gain admission to the Football League failed on two occasions before the Football League expanded from one division to two in 1892, transforming the Football Alliance into the Second Division. There were also a couple of vacancies to be had in the top flight and the Heathens were buoyant at being selected as one of the 'promoted' duo.

Life among the big boys was something of a wake-up call, with Newton Heath finding out that they were not as good as they thought they were and still had some way to go in the football world, as they finished bottom in their first two seasons in the First Division. Saved by a Test Match success in 1893, they failed to win a similar fixture a year later so were relegated to Division Two. Their time at the top had been brief.

Money soon became a problem, not helped by a move to a new ground at Bank Street, Clayton, three miles from their previous home. The support failed to follow, while Bank Street itself was little more than a field of clay with nearby chimneys belching out odious fumes to all and sundry. As one century blended into another, the club was on its last legs, a bazaar was arranged in the hope to raise much needed funds, but much more than that was required.

As legend has it, a St Bernard dog, owned by club captain Harry Stafford took leave of the bazaar and wandered off finding its way to the vicinity of local brewery mogul John H. Davies. One thing led to another and Davies took an interest in the failing football club, clearing the £2,500 debts with a loan of £3,000 and becoming chairman. As this is not a history lesson on Newton Heath nor Manchester United, we will simply leave how Davies became involved with the club at that...

A meeting at the New Islington Public Hall in Ancoats on the evening of Thursday April 24th 1902 was to bring about the end of Newton Heath Football Club, but it also saw the birth of Manchester United when five business men, including club captain Harry Stafford, "promised to subscribe £1,000 each".

Starting afresh was certainly the way ahead and Mr J. Brown, who was chairing the meeting, put forward the proposition of a change of name, adding that it had been mentioned to him in the past that one or two clubs had been late in arriving at the ground, as they had headed towards the Newton Heath area of the city, thinking that due to the name of the club that this was where they were located. He added that any new name had to include 'Manchester' in its title.

Put to a vote, the vast majority of those attending opted for Manchester United and that was that. Although it wasn't quite, as a Football Association enquiry was held in September 1904 into the organisation of the 'new' club and that it was of the opinion that it had been "improperly formed by the sole assistance of Mr Davies", even although he was not aware of the position in which he was being placed. The club were told that they "must be placed on a proper base in the near future".

That initial season under the name Manchester United finished with the club in fifth place in the Second Division, certainly an improvement on 15th and 10th in the previous two, but somewhat strangely, considering the financial burden surrounding the club one place below 4th they had achieved in the seasons 1897-98 to 1899-1900 and the runners-up spot they managed in 1896-97, missing out on promotion due to defeat at the hands of Sunderland in the end of season test matches.

In charge of United at this time was James West, who had held the position of secretary for three years, but despite the turnaround in fortune, he tendered his resignation on Tuesday September 29th, saying:

"Although having every confidence that once settled down the team would justify the care and attention which it has received - a confidence reinforced by the results of the Glossop and Bradford matches - I am not unmindful that my name may be associated with the failure of several of the newer members of the club to sustain the high reputations they had previously gained in first-class football; and solely with a view of relieving the executive of the dub from embarrassment I have decided place the resignation of the secretaryship into the hands the members the board."

Newspapers of the time mentioned that two players who had been 'discharged' by United, Sandy Robertson along with his namesake Tom Robertson but had since been 'pardoned' and were back in training with the club. Had West advocated the dismissal of Robertson for offences that he considered worthy of dismissal only to find himself later over-ruled by his directors? No matter what, he paid the price with his job - under the guidance of West, United had finish 10th, 15th and 5th in the Second Division. They were undistinguished campaigns, although 1902-03 had seen a notable FA Cup run that saw the club through three qualifying rounds and an intermediate round before a 3-1 defeat by Everton in round two.

Season 1903-04 had begun far from favourably with one point from the first three games – drawing 2-2 with Bristol City on the opening day of the season, then losing 2-0 at Burnley and 1-0 at Burslem Port Vale. But suddenly the sun shone through the gloom with a 5-0 victory over Glossop, followed by a further two points from a 3-1 win against Bradford City. Despite those two defeats, United still found themselves in a favourable position – 7th, three points behind leaders Woolwich Arsenal and second-placed Preston North End, although both clubs had a game in hand.

Into the breach came James Ernest Mangnall, with the United directors hoping that the former Burnley man could turn things around. A correspondent with the *Sporting Chronicle* was of the opinion that Mangnall would have not have the financial problems he had endured with the almost bankrupt Burnley. *"He will have no need to exercise such strict economy at Clayton, but for all that, the affairs of the United will not be one with less studiously attended to. If Mr Mangnall can only turn the costly Manchester United team into a winning side he will indeed be a valuable acquisition."*

The position that Mangnall took up with Manchester United, was light years away from what is expected of a football manager today and was more often than not termed 'secretary/manager'. As mentioned elsewhere, Mangnall was not averse to removing his jacket, rolling up his sleeves and cutting the grass, or even other non-documented, perhaps menial tasks, around the pitch. He certainly wasn't expected to toil and sweat around Clayton, although there was plenty that needed doing, nor was he simply just the man who picked the team and oversaw the training. Indeed, his secretarial duties would be much more demanding and certainly time consuming than those in his managerial capacity, as everything to do with the club would fall into his lap. His hours would be long, but would they be fruitful? Only time would tell.

Mangnall needed to judge the players that he had inherited and his first opportunity came with a visit to table-topping Woolwich Arsenal before he took full charge of the team. The directors picked a team that featured four changes to the side that had taken the points off Bradford City the previous weekend, yet it was a far from ideal start as Arsenal registered four without reply, although for some in the press box, they considered that United did not play as well as they had in some of their previous fixtures.

The game attracted a record gate of over 20,000, with many who were present hoping to witness some form of revenge for the two defeats that United had inflicted on Arsenal the previous season. They might have had their doubts as to the eventual outcome in the opening quarter, as it was United who were the better of the two sides, but as the half time whistle blew, the home side held a one goal lead. Play in the second half became quite physical at times, but Arsenal continued their fine vein of recent form, adding three more goals and taking their total for the season to twenty-one from five fixtures, with none conceded, they were top of the Second Division and would be promoted at the end of the season, United on the other hand could only look to improve.

Improve they certainly did, reversing the 4-0 score line from Plumstead seven days previously with a fine victory over Barnsley at Clayton, with goals from centre-half Griffiths, his sixth of the season, the recently suspended Sandy Robertson and a couple from centre-forward Pegg. It wasn't all one-way traffic during the ninety minutes, as the *Athletic News* correspondent considered that United "won and deserved to win, but not by four goals". It could have been five as Downie missed a penalty, while at the opposite end United's reserve team goalkeeper Harry Moger, making his debut and in place of Sutcliffe who was on Football League duty, did his prospects no harm at all by saving a penalty.

Goals had proved something of a problem for United

during the campaign despite scoring five against Glossop and the four against Barnsley, as six of the first eleven fixtures had seen the attack fail to register. Three of the four fixtures that followed that victory over Barnsley were amongst the blanks – two 0-0 draws at Lincoln City and at home to Bolton Wanderers and a 2-0 defeat at home to Preston North End. A 3-1 win against Stockport County sandwiched in between the two draws.

The home defeat to Preston was far from a disgrace because their Lancashire neighbours were unbeaten in the league this season, but what was a disappointment to Mangnall and the United officials was the disappointing 15,000 crowd, considering that home fixtures against Bristol City, Bradford City, Barnsley and Bolton Wanderers had attracted 40,000, 30,000, 20,000 and 30,000 respectively. Only Stockport County's visit to Clayton attracted around the same as the Preston fixture, which was not surprising as they sat at the foot of the table.

For Mangnall especially, the poor crowds were a huge disappointment, as not only was there a special train from Preston leaving the town at 9.47am and another at 1.00pm but special electric cars were operating between the Cromwell monument close to Manchester Cathedral and only a short walk from Victoria Station, and the Clayton ground at a charge of twopence. The latter of the two special trains would take the supporters past Victoria to Park Station, which was not far from the ground. In its travel details for the match, the *Lancashire Daily Post* added: *"The United enclosure is now one of the finest in the country, and has covered accommodation for 20,000 people without any additional charge beyond the sixpence entrance."* Some who attended the ground on a regular basis, might not have held a similar opinion!

The Preston defeat was something of a rare occurrence, not just amid the back-drop of Clayton's belching chimneys but as United travelled round the grounds of their Second Division opponents. The 'Manchester United nil' tag was also dispensed with as only two other fixtures that season, the penultimate ninety minutes at Bolton Wanderers and their FA Cup second round tie against Sheffield Wednesday, saw United fail to score.

Three of the next quartet of fixtures, following the 2-0 defeat by Preston North End on November 21st, ended in 1-1 draws, all against Small Heath in the FA Cup intermediate round. There could well have been another two defeats sandwiched in between, but the league fixture against Grimsby Town in late November was abandoned due to bad light, with Grimsby leading 2-1, then early December saw the home fixture against Leicester Fosse abandoned due to fog. So with only two partly completed fixtures and Small Heath's visit to Manchester on December 5th on FA Cup business, United could have been considered somewhat rusty.

Managing to secure a replay against Small Heath, thanks to a Schofield goal, some 6,000 turned up at the Coventry Road Grounds in Birmingham, expecting the home side to progress into the next round, but again United came from behind and forced the game into extra time, both sides missing penalties and although reduced to ten men due to an injury to Downie, United held on to take the tie into a third game at Bramall Lane, Sheffield.

Before that third meeting could take place, United got back to winning ways with a 4-2 victory over Gainsborough Trinity, but it mattered little, as once again, the game ended all-square. Once again a penalty kick was missed, Sutcliffe keeping United in the game, but as in the previous meetings Small Heath took the lead, only to see United deny them victory with an equaliser and so a third replay was required but the next instalment in the saga would not be played until January. By then United had overcome Chesterfield 3-1, and a point was taken off Burton United and Bristol City with a 2—2 draw and a 1-1 draw respectively, all of which left the reds in sixth position in the Second Division table with nineteen points, thirteen adrift of leaders Preston North End, but having played three games fewer. Bolton, in third, were seven points better off but had played five games more. Second placed Arsenal had played two games more and had a ten point advantage. The possibility of promotion wasn't exactly out of the question. The prolonged FA Cup tie against Small Heath was finally decided at Manchester City's Hyde Road ground, and on this occasion there was no need for extra time, nor a United fight-back. Grassam gave United the lead in the opening half and although they enjoyed the bulk of the play, it wasn't until the final five minutes of the game that the outcome was made certain, Arkesden scoring twice, before Athersmith grabbed a consolation for Small Heath.

A chance for Mangnall to assess the team's progress came on the last Saturday of January 1904 when Woolwich Arsenal visited Clayton. On the morning of the game, a correspondent for the *Manchester Courier and Lancashire General Advertiser* wrote:

> *"The match of the season at Clayton par excellence will be witnessed there to-day, when Manchester United entertain Woolwich Arsenal. The 'Gunners' realise that the United supply the most dangerous opposition to their long-cherished wish of securing*

> *promotion, and thereby introducing First Division football to the South of England. While the match is exciting the greatest interest in Manchester and district, Londoners are in a like degree affected, and the special trains which are being run from the Metropolis will no doubt convey large number of people North who will do their utmost to urge the Woolwich Reds on victory. On the other hand, we have the authority of Mr. Mangnall, the energetic secretary the United Club, for stating that the players and officials recognise the vital importance of the match, and that a big effort will be made to achieve success. It is fully expected that the players will rise to the occasion, and thus give their supporters some ground for hoping that they will operate in the First Division next season. A defeat to-day would practically prove fatal to their chance."*

Sensing the importance of the occasion, some forty odd thousand converged on Clayton and although some might have been disappointed in not being rewarded with more than one goal, that it was scored by United's Sandy Robertson certainly made up for seeing the back of the net bulge only once. Much was made of United's victory, and indeed Arsenal's defeat, with the *London Daily News* lamenting:

> *"By losing to Manchester United on Saturday, the Arsenal allowed their opponents to creep to within five points of themselves. It is not a matter of surprise that the Woolwich eleven should have gone under, for the United are an equally determined and capable team. The defeat in itself would not be very serious but for the fact that it meant a*

*difference of four points, the spoils of the game
going, as they did, to the Arsenal's most formidable
rivals. The situation of the Woolwich club is now
critical. Preston North End have the championship
of the division in safe keeping, with 12 games to
play, only in those against Manchester United at
Deepdale and the Arsenal at Plumstead can the
results be looked upon with uncertainty.*

*"Therefore, there is but one position in the
market. Manchester United will bid for it 'regardless
of cost,' and whilst they have as good a team as
the Arsenal at present, they have a much longer
purse. How deadly in earnest are the Manchester
team may be gathered from the fact that 45,000
people turned out to encourage them on Saturday.
The Arsenal's promotion would be widely popular,
but not more so than that of the United, who have
not only the Lancashire clubs, but the influence of
Mr. J. J. Bentley, Chairman of the League, behind
them. Mr. Bentley is also chairman of Manchester
United and though he may be depended upon
not to usurp his position, he may be expected to
use every legitimate means towards the United's
promotion. Of course, Woolwich, with a lead of
five points, hold the whip hand, but unless they
improve upon recent performances - in the result
they will be overhauled."*

There was no mention, however, of J. E. Mangnall's
contribution to United's good form. The victory over
Arsenal certainly narrowed the gap, they were now only
five points behind the 'Gunners' with a game in hand,
but any boost received from that victory did not ensure
success against First Division Notts County in the 1ˢᵗ

round of the FA Cup. A fixture that was put into some doubt prior to kick-off when a rumour circulated that one of the County players had "contracted small-pox, or been in contact with someone suffering from that disease". The club doctor was to examine every County player prior to kick-off and was to declare that the rumour was unfounded and all the players were clear of the disease "at least in its more serious aspect and there was not necessary to order the team into quarantine."

That afternoon United wallowed in the heavy conditions and by all accounts were unlucky not to go straight into the second round draw. Taking the lead after ten minutes through Downie, they were soon pegged back, but were back in front midway through the half when Schofield added a second. Again County managed to equalise, then go in front, but an Arkesden goal took the game to a replay where United progressed into the second round by the odd goal in three, but they became totally unstuck at Hillsborough, conceding six without reply to eventual First Division champions Sheffield Wednesday. United may have been out of the cup but their assault on promotion continued, although a 2-1 reversal at Blackpool on the second Saturday in March, left them in sixth place on twenty-six points, six behind third place Burnley and nine behind second placed Arsenal. Preston North End were galloping over the horizon, fourteen points in front. Such gaps mattered little to Mangnall and his team. Games and points were there to be won and anything was possible.

With promotion a distinct possibility, Mangnall had already started planning for the future and former captain, saviour and chief scout, Harry Stafford, was soon a regular passenger on trains bound for Grimsby. The object of

Stafford's attentions was initially unclear but the *Woolwich Gazette* included in their edition of Friday April 22nd 1904 the intriguing line – *"Perhaps they only wanted to see Roberts at centre-half (?) but surely one visit to Grimsby per week is enough, eh, Mr Stafford."* A day later, which was FA Cup final day, the reason for Harry's regular visits to Blundell Park became clear as headlines confirmed "Grimsby Half-Back Goes to Manchester" – Ernest Mangnall had made his first and arguably most significant move in the transfer market with the capture of twenty-year-old Charlie Roberts, the 5ft 11½in, 12st 6lb centre-half while their main rivals for his signature, Manchester City, were pre-occupied by preparations for the cup final against Bolton. There was little fan-fare, a mere paragraph was the most that the newspapers of the day included as regards the signing, but for Mangnall and Manchester United this was arguably the most important piece of business that the secretary/manager would carry out during tenure at United. Some questioned the reported £600 fee for the Darlington-born pivot whose experience in league football amounted to just 31 appearances but the United directorate trusted Mangnall's opinion and were happy to bankroll the deal.

Roberts made his United debut against Burton United before 8,000 supporters at Clayton on Saturday April 23rd in the third last fixture of the season. United's 2-0 win set up a nail-biting finale, as following that afternoon's results the picture of a few weeks previously had changed, almost beyond recognition, as it was Woolwich Arsenal who sat in pole position in the Second Division table, with forty-eight points from their thirty-three games while Preston North End had floundered and were also on forty-eight points, while United were now a mere three points behind the leading duo with a game in hand. Eight victories, a draw and a defeat had seen the gap almost vanish. Promotion was now a real possibility.

The promotion fight was going to be decided on Lancastrian soil – in the penultimate fixture of the season, United had to lock horns with Mangnall's old club Bolton Wanderers in what was their game in hand, while Preston were to come face to face with Blackpool on the final afternoon. United would bring down their curtain with a visit from Leicester Fosse on that final Saturday. Unfortunately promotion didn't go to that final Saturday afternoon as United drew 0-0 with Bolton allowing Preston North End and Arsenal to join the First Division for the 1904-05 season.

Falling at what was more or less the last hurdle was disappointing, but it showed that bringing Mangnall to Manchester was a good piece of work and achieving third place was far from failure, giving the club something to build on. That was certainly the opinion of the *Manchester Evening News* whose correspondent wrote of the club's prospects for the coming season: *"Although on paper the players available do not appear to be as formidable as some of their well-wishers would wish, yet the officials of the Manchester United Football Club believe that they have got the material necessary to carry them to the top of the Second Division of the League. That the task of carrying off this honour next season will be a great one leaves of no possible doubt whatever, for the junior division of the League looks like being stronger than it has ever been in the past."*

Training for the 1904-05 season began at the end of July while Mangnall and Harry Stafford had overseen the re-laying of several portions of the Clayton pitch, something that was long overdue and although the conditions helped, it was the results that were of ultimate importance and having come so close to achieving promotion at the end of the previous season, a similar campaign, with the hoped for promotion at the end of it, was very much on the agenda.

The season began with a 2-2 draw at Burslem Port Vale, followed by a 4-1 home victory against Bristol City and then something of shock reversal against Bolton Wanderers, also at Clayton. A mixed bag, but it was still early days. As well as having his eyes firmly fixed on the playing side of the club, Mangnall, having been in business himself, maintained a keen interest in all aspects of Manchester United and he was always eyeing an opportunity to boost the coffers. Drinking in the ground while watching the match was a popular pastime as following the recent fixture against Bristol City it had been noted that a considerable number of empty bottles had been left behind by the 20,000 crowd, so it was decided to apply for an 'occasional licence' to cover the game against Bolton Wanderers and also some thirty-three or thirty-four other Saturdays during the season, with the licence being given to Mangnall's predecessor James West, now licensee of the Union Hotel in Princess Street.

It was argued that the application was being put forward due to public demand as it was during the quarter of an hour interval that some of the spectators wanted refreshments. Between 25,000 and 30,000 were there every Saturday and with Bolton in town, excursion trains would more than likely be running, bringing in a number of visitors.

An application had been made the previous week, and refused, with Mangnall stating that a large number of empty bottles were found after the game. When asked if they had contained lemonade or milk, he replied "no". It was also reported that there had been more disturbance and drunkenness the previous Saturday than there had been for the past twelve months. There was a bar within the ground, but if spectators found it too busy, they asked for a pass out to go elsewhere for a drink and then return. Against Bristol City, it was estimated that some 2,000 wanted to go out, which was impossible to manage, while it was noted that there were a lot more intoxicated people in the vicinity of the ground after the game than normal. This was considered to be due to people bringing bottles and jugs of beer into the ground and drinking more than they would if there had simply been another bar with the ground. If a license was granted, then the second bar would be under a stand which was yet to be erected. There were also fifteen policemen and the same number of other attendants present on a match day to keep order.

Still, the license was refused.

Many left Clayton at full-time on September 17th and went off to drown their sorrows following a 2-1 defeat against Bolton Wanderers but it would be February 11th, and an away fixture at Lincoln City, before defeat in the league would be tasted again. Yet despite that long and unbroken sequence of victories, mainly thanks to the goals of Arkesden, that top of the table position remained impossible to acquire, due to the similar rich vein of form maintained by Liverpool and Bolton Wanderers. On the morning of that 3-0 reversal at Lincoln, United were second, two points behind Bolton, but with two games in hand, Liverpool were third, having played a game fewer than United. One other thing that United had in their favour was that their interest in the FA Cup had ended at the first hurdle, losing to Fulham by a solitary goal following two draws.

Mangnall's footballing beliefs stretched far and wide. He was described as a "painstaking official" in the *Athletic News* and without any shadow of doubt, he now had United on track for promotion. Although having competent trainers at the club in renowned middle-distance runner F.E. Bacon and his assistant Nuttall, an old friend and colleague at Bolton, he was more often than not there to supervise. Although a keen devotee of practise making perfect, Mangnall also saw benefit in relaxation prior to fixtures and with a heavy holiday programme looming as 1904 moved into 1905, he took his players off to Fairhaven, close to Lytham St Anne's "to inhale the sea breezes which are so invigorating." Whether it was that fresh sea air, the fish and chips or the delights of nearby Blackpool, it is not documented, but whatever it was, it certainly invigorated the United players, especially in the final League game of 1904 and opening fixture of 1905 which produced resounding victories – 6-1 against Burslem Port Vale and 7-0 [a record score] against Bradford City.

An article in the *Lancashire Evening Post* in November spoke of the team as playing "high-class football", with "a reliable man for every position", with the latter also applicable to J. E. Mangnall, but that December a scandal rocked United when Mangnall's predecessor James West and former captain, now director, Harry Stafford were found guilty of being "cognisant of illegal payments having been made to players and that proper accounts were not kept" by an F.A. enquiry. Stafford had played a central role in salvaging the club from the ashes of Newton Heath, while West had been United's first secretary but now they and it was also found that the club was "not properly constituted or carried on as set forth in a previous report." The pair were suspended from football and football management until May 1st 1907.

Defeat to Fulham in the intermediate round of the F.A. Cup, whilst disappointing, allowed the club to focus on promotion, but those hopes were to take something of a knock in February with a trio of fixtures producing one victory, one draw and one defeat. Had the draw and defeat resulted in victories then United would have found themselves in a much more challenging position to Second Division leaders Bolton Wanderers, but as it was, they found themselves five points behind with two games in hand.

The 3-0 defeat at Lincoln City and the 0-0 draw at Burnley were the first games that the United front line had failed to register in since the season began excluding the two cup-ties against Fulham, and they were not to be the last, as another goalless draw at Gainsborough Trinity in early April, sandwiched by a 6-0 win over Doncaster Rovers and a 5-0 victory at Clayton against Burton United, did little to help that promotion push, as on the morning of the game, United were level on forty-eight points with Bolton Wanderers and Liverpool, the goal average of the trio being almost identical, but following that 0-0 draw, top spot had been relinquished to Liverpool.

Following a 5-0 win over Burton United on April 15th, with three games remaining, it was everything to play for. Liverpool remained on top – fifty-two points from their thirty-one games. Bolton Wanderers were second with an identical number of points from their thirty-one games – Liverpool had scored two more, but conceded five fewer. United were third, a point behind.

Up until March Mangnall had held little reason to stop and change his team as the results flowed freely, but against Barnsley on the last day of February, he found himself without full-backs Hayes and Bonthron, centre-half Charlie Roberts and outside-right Schofield. It was perhaps of little surprise that a point was dropped. It is also perhaps not much of surprise that with various changes to the line-up in that final quarter of the season, vital points were subsequently dropped.

Mangnall made his changes, forced or otherwise, with one paying huge dividends, the introduction of former Newton Heath Athletic player Dick Duckworth, who had joined the club as a half-back in 1903 but who had made only two previous league appearances at right-half, but was now drafted in as a makeshift centre-forward, scoring one against Grimsby Town, a hat-trick against Doncaster Rovers and a double against Burton United. That 5-0 victory should have been the launch-pad for a final assault on the championship, or at the very least, promotion as runners-up, but it was to prove fatal.

The finale to that 1904-05 season came amid three games in the same number of days – Chesterfield away on April 21st, Liverpool away on April 22nd and Blackpool at home on April 24th. However, there was little need for all three fixtures to be played, one was enough.

On Saturday April 22nd, United lost 2-0 at Saltergate while Liverpool defeated Doncaster Rovers 1-0 and Bolton Wanderers scored two against Blackpool without reply. United were three points behind the leaders. If that defeat at Chesterfield didn't kill off the promotion hopes, then the subsequent 4-0 reversal at Anfield was the final nail in the coffin with the 3-1 victory over Blackpool on the final day nothing more than a thank you to the home support. United had finished third for the second consecutive season.

Despite the disappointment no fingers were pointed at Mangnall, according to the *Manchester Evening News*, he had *"discharged his duties of secretary in a most thorough and capable manner, succeeded in inducing the Burton officials to part with Beddow and in the hope of improving the men, about fourteen weeks were spent in special training at Fairhaven, and Mr. Mangnall added to his good work in securing the help of Wombwell."* The paper also considered it to be "bad luck" rather than "bad play" that had seen their promotion hopes collapse.

4: PROMOTION AT LAST

THE DISAPPOINTMENT OF a second successive third place was soon shrugged off and no sooner had the curtain come down on the 1904-05 season than Mangnall was planning for the next campaign. *"Manchester United F.C. Invite Applications From First Class Players For Next Season"* was the advert in the *Athletic News* of Monday May 1st 1905, which included: *"Particulars, stating age, Height, weight and clubs played for, to J.E. Mangnall, Secretary, Bank Street, Clayton, Manchester."*

Such an advert was far from uncommon as others, not quite so bold as United's, also appeared. Tottenham Hotspur were looking for a *"First class right-back"*, West Bromwich Albion sought *"first class players for next season"*, West Ham United wanted a *"first class inside-left"*, Liverpool wanted *"players for all positions"*, while a goalkeeper, back, left-half and inside-right were wanted by a *"First Division League team."* It wasn't only players who were sought, but also groundsmen, while individual players would also put themselves in the marketplace – *"Joe Schofield, Outside Right, is open for engagement; just finished two seasons with Manchester United; age 22 – Best terms to 246, Old Road, Ashton-in-Makerfield, near Wigan."*

The success of these advertisements is open to question, suffice to say that by the middle of that month Bury had been relieved of their goalkeeper Archie Montgomery and forward Charlie Sagar. Both players were happy with the terms offered to them by the United secretary and in the knowledge that they would be playing Second

Division football, but there was suddenly the prospect that United could find themselves playing in the top flight. At the Annual Meeting of the Football League in London on Monday May 29th, Mr. C.E. Sutcliffe proposed that the League be increased to forty clubs, from the current thirty-six, stating that the weaker clubs financially required all the assistance they could get, whilst adding; *"Who the two clubs were to be which entered the first League he did not care."* He also felt that the league would benefit by increased numbers. However, things were not exactly straight forward as an anonymous circular, which was strongly condemned by many, had been distributed speaking out against the proposal, yet despite this and seven clubs voting against it, a show of hands carried the proposal.

A series of votes would decide which new clubs would enter the Second Division and it was agreed that the following clubs should apply for the two First Division vacancies: Bury, Bristol City. Manchester United, Notts County and West Bromwich Albion. Bury and Notts County had finished in the bottom two places at the end of the 1904-05 season, but how West Bromwich Albion managed to get a place in the mix is anyone's guess as they were one of the clubs who voted against the proposal! So, it went to the vote. Bury received 32, Notts County 33, United 13, Bristol City 9 and the Albion 3.

Although it might seem cut and dried it didn't quite end there as Mr. Maley of Manchester City, *"indignantly protested against the imputation made by some persons in the room that the scurrilous circular which had been issued in reference to the proposal had mandated from his club. As to the suggestion that Manchester City was antagonistic to Manchester United, so far from that being the case had nominations been necessary he would have been prepared to nominate Manchester United to the First Division."*

The matter didn't simply die a death, as it simmered away below the surface for a few weeks, raising a few eyebrows in the process. An article in the *Bristol Times and Mirror* on Saturday July 8th read: *"Why did not Manchester United not get elected into the First Division after their president had been so indefatigable in bringing about the extension of the First Division for it is whispered at any rate, their especial benefit? The question has been asked of Mr. Cry himself repeatedly and he says with reference to it: 'All I know is that the secretary, Mr. Mangnall, obtained 31 promises, and that over 20 representatives of clubs assured him they had voted for the United, in expressing their regret, and yet only 13 votes were recorded. Obviously Mr. Mangnall had somehow mixed up his 31 and transposed the figures into 13, or someone was not adhering strictly to the truth. Under the circumstances, I quite agree that the Manchester United were justified in feeling disappointed: but Rome was not built in a day, and the United will make another struggle.'"*

First Division fare would have been welcomed with open arms, but if it was going to be achieved it was through results rather than a show of hands. Having finished the previous two seasons within touching distance of promotion, Mangnall, his directors and his players were very much aware as to what had to be done to make that final step up into the top division. They had also noticed that climbing to the top of that tree was not an impossibility either, as Liverpool had gone from winning the Second Division title in 1904-05 to claiming the First Division crown twelve months later. If they could do it, then why not Manchester United?

Six straight wins kick-started the 1905-06 season, an emphatic 5-1 hammering of Bristol City on the opening day making United's intentions clear to all. Mangnall's decision to take his players to Northwich to enjoy the luxury of their brine baths, something that he had considered beneficial during the previous season, was already paying dividends.

Charlie Sagar immediately proved Mangnall's decision to lure him away from near neighbours Bury as being a shrewd piece of business, scoring twice on that opening afternoon, while another new addition to the squad, Jack Picken, who Mangnall knew from his Bolton days and had joined from Plymouth Argyle at the end of the previous season, also scored while another master-stroke saw Charlie Roberts named as captain.

Although they had challenged for promotion over the course of the previous two seasons, the name 'Manchester United' had rarely sat atop the Second Division but with half a dozen games played there they were sitting proudly in poll position, with a two-point lead over Bristol City and a healthy goal average, having scored three more and conceded six fewer than the Robins. It wasn't going to be plain sailing however as there would be defeats at some point along the way as well as other obstacles to overcome, while, as could be expected, opponents were certainly not going to give away any unnecessary advantage and would fight until the final whistle to prevent United securing victory.

Whether there was any animosity towards Mangnall's team, or indeed dislike toward Manchester United in general owing to their growing superiority, is up for debate, but feelings certainly ran high on Saturday September 30th when United travelled to Blackpool. The ninety minutes produced a closely fought encounter, with a Charlie Roberts goal all that separated the teams as the final whistle blew but as the referee signalled the end of the game, it was to produce a reaction from a few disgruntled members in the 7,000-strong Bloomfield Road crowd. During the ninety minutes, and more so towards the end of the game, referee Fred Kirkham had to be at the top of his game to keep a tight hold on the players, while along the touchline, sections of the crowd were becoming distinctly agitated and excited, as Blackpool pushed, in vain as it turned out, for an equaliser.

As the players were leaving the field, a number of people gathered around the entrance area to the dressing rooms and Connor of Blackpool, who had received a knee injury during the game, struck out at Bonthron, the United right-back. Mangnall at once seized the arm of his defender in order to prevent any form of retaliation, while the referee took Connor into the dressing room. The official also noted the name of a spectator as Bonthron was escorted to the visitor's dressing room by a police officer. It later transpired that other United players had been assaulted as they left the pitch. Somewhat surprisingly, little more was heard of the incident.

A goalless draw against Bradford City at Clayton on October 7th saw the first point of the season dropped and a further two followed a week later when West Bromwich Albion inflicted a 1-0 defeat at the Hawthorns, two results that left many wondering if United's early season bubble had burst. The *Leeds Mercury* of Monday October 16th contained the following:

> *"For the past week or so it has been noticed that Manchester United have been going backward, the front rank in particular showing signs of deterioration, and at last they have suffered defeat. As illustrating the keenness of the struggle which is*

taking place at the top of the Second League, though the Mancunians have only lost three points out of eight matches, they have bid to vacate the position of honour, which is now occupied by Bristol City with fourteen points out of eight engagements. To be beaten by an odd goal at West Bromwich is not a very bad performance, but still the United were not seen to be their best."

Mangnall soon had things back on track with a 3-2 victory over Leicester Fosse, but a further dropped point at Gainsborough Trinity in a 2-2 draw and another defeat, this time at Chesterfield, coupled with victories over Hull and Lincoln, proved to the rest of the Second Division clubs that United were far from unbeatable. That 1-0 defeat at Chesterfield on November 11th allowed Bristol City to take a two point advantage at the top of the table, whilst also having the advantage of a game in hand. Had the *Leeds Mercury* got it right? Were United going to suffer a run of negative results and performances?

No chance: Mangnall cajoled his men into a swift return to form and they bounced back with not only victories, but goals – 3-0 against Burslem Port Vale and Barnsley as November was marked off the calendars. Then it was 4-0 at home to Clapton Orient, 3-1 at Burnley and a 2-0 victory two days before Christmas against Burton United. "They were not seen at their best" reported the *Athletic News* of the Burton game, but the run of results kept them in contention for promotion, although not propelling them to the top of the table. Only two points separated them from Bristol City, with both clubs having played the same number of games, but there was now a gap of five points between second and third.

As 1905 drew to a close, third-place Chelsea left

Clayton on Christmas Day with a point from a goalless draw, while Charlie Roberts rescued a point in the top of the table clash against Bristol City on December 30th. It was a goal, and a point, that would prove vital in that title challenge – had United lost to the league leaders then they would have been five points adrift, albeit with a game in hand, as they moved into the second half of the season.

It was back into the swing of things during the cold afternoons of January 1906; Grimsby Town conceding five without reply in the first fixture of the year before it was onto FA Cup business. The cup had held little in the way of success for either Manchester United or Newton Heath and despite a more than promising start to the 1906 competition – a 7-2 victory over Staple Hill, followed by two further home victories, 3-0 against Norwich City and 5-1 against Aston Villa, they were to come unstuck against Woolwich Arsenal in an enthralling ninety minutes, again at Clayton, which the visitors won by the odd goal in five.

It was early March by the time interest in the FA Cup was finally extinguished by which time the Second Division table had taken on a new look. A 3-0 defeat at Leeds City had knocked the wind out of United sails a little but Mangnall managed to get his team back on track with relative ease and following that Yorkshire reversal Glossop paid the price with a 5-2 hammering and Stockport were beaten by the only goal of the game.

Perhaps the most controversial game in United's brief history to that point had occurred on Saturday February 10th when they crossed the Pennines to face Bradford City. Despite the 5-1 score line in United's favour, the Bantams had enjoyed their share of the play, although had the United front-line been on song the difference between the sides could have been greater. Determining the actual goal scorers in some of those fixtures from the distant past can be a minefield. Take that Bradford City match for example as the newspapers and records vary between – Beddow 2, Roberts, Wombwell and Schofield to Picken notching the first and Beddow only scoring one, to Bell scoring the first and again Beddow scoring one. No matter who scored that opening goal, the five put past Bradford goalkeeper Daw did not go down well with the home support and a re-enactment of a scene from the Wars of the Roses was played out at full-time.

The story was soon splashed across newspapers nationwide: "Another Mobbing Affair – Manchester United Attacked" – *The Sheffield Evening Telegraph*; "Exciting Scenes At Bradford – Manchester Players Roughly Treated By The Crowd" – *Lancashire Evening Post*;"Football Players Stoned"– *Aberdeen Press and Journal*; "Football Disturbance At Bradford" – *Edinburgh Evening News*; "Football Mobbing At Bradford – Manchester Players Under Police Protection" – *Leeds Mercury* were just a selection of the headlines following those ninety minutes at Bradford, with correspondents from the newspapers covering the full time scenes at Valley Parade in great detail.

From the *Sheffield Evening Telegraph:*

> *"A remarkable and regrettable scene, which may have serious consequences for the Bradford City Club, took place after the match with Manchester United at Valley Parade. Long before the finish it was obvious that a disorderly section of the spectators were in an ugly humour. After the players had dressed, a man is said to have struck Bonthron,*

and it is said that this person was seized by a Bradford official and detained. To reach vehicles the Manchester players had to walk up a narrow thoroughfare leading to the main road. Here it was that people congregated, and the appearance of the United players outside ground was the signal for hooting and an angry demonstration. Bonthron was escorted by police, and a number of the Bradford officials and players, and several his own comrades.

"Mud was thrown, until Bonthron's clothes were splashed from head to foot. In some cases, stones are said to have been flung, and at least one person was struck. Finally Bonthron was escorted into the yard of the Belle Vue Hotel by his friends. Here he entered a cab and Mr. P. O'Rourke (secretary of the Bradford City Club), seating himself on the box the vehicle was driven through the crowd. The other Manchester players and officials followed in cabs, and a stone was hurled through the window of the conveyance in which the President of the Football League. Mr. J. J. Bentley, the secretary to the Manchester United Club Mr. E. Mangnall; and Mr. J. Taylor, a member of the committee."

The *Bradford Weekly Telegraph*, although not completely biased towards the local side, did add oddments of criticism to their match summary that were missing from the others, although to their credit, as if they had much of an option, said that the scenes were "very regrettable". Their correspondent wrote about the crowd becoming:

"...very excited over questionable tactics indulged in by the visitors, and yelled their disapproval. Probably the fact that the visitors had scored three

times early on in the game had a good deal to do with the felling of the crowd for the home team supporters had been pretty confident that the Manchester club would go under and when the rough play followed the crowd was furious. The Manchester player who came in for the greatest share of the public displeasure was Bonthron, the right-back, and the manner in which he met the advances of Conlin, the City left wing forward, first gave rise to disapprobation.

"Apart from the fact that it was the home team's forward which had the worst of the encounters and got 'laid out' two or three times, the fact that he was the smallest and lightest player on the field gained him the sympathy of the spectators. The referee also gained the disapproval of the crowd by several of his decisions, but it was hardly expected that any resentment would be shown after the match was over and the players and officials were allowed to leave the field without interference."

Speaking to the *Daily Mail*, Mr. J.J. Bentley, the Football League President, gave a slightly different view of the performance of the match official and Bonthron, saying:

"The Manchester United players and the referee Mr. Campbell of Blackburn, had an unpleasant experience after the match. A large portion of the crowd remained on the ground near to the dressing tents, and were continually calling for the referee and Bonthron. The exact cause of the complaint was not very apparent, as the referee had not been called upon to decide any vital point, and the

United had won by five goals to one.

"As for Bonthron, he played his usually vigorous game, but, with the single exception of fouling Conlin in the second half, the referee had no reason to complain. Mr. Brunt and other members of the Bradford Committee endeavoured to take Bonthron out by a side entrance, but were met by a hostile crowd, and on Mr Brunt returning outside, he was, although wearing the official Bradford badge, struck violently in the back of the neck.

"It was then considered advisable to return and go out by the usual exit, and Bonthron had a very unpleasant experience, being badly kicked going up the incline leading to the main street, while he was covered with mud, and, but for the prompt action of the police, who rushed him into the Belle Vue Hotel, would have been seriously molested. The referee had a rough time, stones being thrown at him and his pipe knocked out of his mouth; while like Bonthron, he was covered in mud."

"You can't imagine what it was like," Charlie Roberts said later, "I have never experienced anything like it. I pushed several men away who were going for Bonthron. I was glad to get out of it."

Having filled countless column inches in the Monday morning editions of the national press, the events at Valley Parade didn't disappear and continued in various forms over the next few days. Tuesday February 13th produced a copy a letter from Mangnall, who had been struck with a missile but was uninjured, to his opposite number at Bradford City – Mr P. O'Rourke.

It read: "Dear O'Rourke, Our directors desire

me to express extreme regret at the unpleasant proceedings which took place our match on Saturday. They were disgraceful. At the same time, they wish to exonerate your directors, and, indeed, beg to thank them most heartily for the steps they took to protect the members out team and officials. Yours truly. J. E. MANGNALL. February 11th, 1906."

With the events at Bradford still smouldering away and unlikely to disappear anytime soon, United, or more to the point Mangnall and his fellow officials, suddenly found themselves in the news and fingers pointed in their direction when they were accused of "sordid commercialism".

In the build-up to their F.A. Cup tie against Aston Villa at Clayton on February 24th, they decided to make the lowest admission fee one shilling. In an attempt to justify this decision, they said that *"all parts of the ground was acceptable to the paying public on the one basis"*. All well and good, but the *Daily Mirror* argued that *"they are not considering their best patron, the working man, who uncomplainingly pays his sixpence, and attends, whatever the weather be. No club in the kingdom has been better supported by the real working-class than Manchester United, and it is nothing less than a scandal that the very men who have made the club what it is, should be practically fined for seeing their own club figure at home in an important cup-tie."*

Following a goalless draw at West Brom on the Saturday, Tuesday February 20th saw the committee appointed to inquire into the disturbance meet at the Great Northern Hotel in Bradford and it was something of a full-house, with all the Bradford City directors present, along with players Robinson, Carter and Conlin. From United,

along with Mangnall, came Roberts and Bonthron, with
Football League President J.J. Bentley and the referee and
linesmen also there to add some weight to proceedings.
The four-man committee took two and a half hours
hearing the evidence, during which time Mangnall and
the referee were allowed to remain in the room and
also question witnesses. During the proceedings, one of
the Bradford players, commented on the tactics of the
United players and stated that the penalty area should
be *"considerably enlarged in order to make the punishment for
fouls more severe"*. There was never any real doubt that
the referee and the United players had been assaulted
and the enquiry was more or less called to decide what
punishment should be handed out and at the end of the
meeting, Bradford City were ordered that their ground to
be closed for fourteen days.

The 'Battle of Bradford' was soon forgotten and the F.A.
Cup was also relegated to the memory bank as a five-
goal Bank Street salvo saw off Hull City. While United
were pre-occupied with cup business others had taken
advantage and the Second Division table on the night of
March 10th saw Bristol City still leading the pack with
fifty points from twenty-nine games, Chelsea were now
in second place with forty-four points from the same
number of games, while United had been knocked back
into third spot with forty-three points from twenty-seven
games. Two victories from their games in hand would
push them back onto the shoulder of the leaders but if
Bristol City kept winning then Chelsea were the team
they had to keep a close eye on. The Londoners were the
only one of that rival duo who United had still to face.

Scoring five goals on five occasions between January
6th and March 3rd displayed the capabilities of Mangnall's

men, both as individuals and as a team, however, it remains a mystery how United could go from scoring five one Saturday, to only scoring once seven days later, bouncing back with another five the following Saturday, then failing to score at all before scoring five in both of their next two fixtures. That, however, is what they did. But those individual performances and five goal victories, while lauded by the Clayton management and support, were not always accepted at other venues. In the final two fixtures of March United scored a 5-2 victory over Leicester Fosse and a 5-1 success against Barnsley. Six points now separated United and Bristol City, but if the two games in hand were won, then the battle for the championship was well and truly on. That championship was in effect out of United's hands as winning all their remaining fixtures promised nothing, unless that was, Bristol City dropped points.

There was a glimmer of hope around Clayton at tea time on Saturday April 7th as news filtered through that Bristol City had drawn 2-2 at Burnley, while a solitary George Wall goal had been enough to secure both points at Clapton Orient. But it was back to square one six days later as the Easter programme got underway, as United drew 1-1 with Chelsea, while Bristol City defeated Gainsborough Trinity 2-0, and they repeated the scoreline in their following two fixtures against Leeds City and Grimsby Town. United replied with wins against Burnley [1-0] and Gainsborough Trinity [2-0]. The leaders had two games left, United had three but with the Bristol side having held that top position for so long it appeared unlikely that they would relinquish it now. Chelsea, in third, also had to be content with that Mangnall's men were unlikely to throw anything away at this stage of the season.

As it was, Bristol City defeated Burton United 1-0 and Chelsea 2-1 to secure the title, while United completed their fixture list with victories against Leeds City [3-1], Lincoln City [3-2] and Burton United [6-0]. It was disappointing not to be crowned champions, but the aim for the club throughout the season had been promotion and this had been achieved. Manchester United were now a First Division club.

The 6-0 win over Burton United at Clayton on April 28th was a fitting 'au-revoir' to the Second Division, while also being a message of intent to the First Division that they were certainly not coming to make up the numbers. As the full-time whistle brought down the curtain on the 1905-06 season, many of the 16,000 crowd invaded the pitch, with the players carried shoulder high towards the dressing rooms. A 'pyrotechnic display', accompanied by the music of the St Joseph's Industrial School Band added colour to the occasion.

Having allowed the jubilant players to access the dressing rooms, the crowd then congregated in front of the stand, where they remained for over an hour cheering and calling for the triumphant players and officials. In time club President Mr. J.H. Davies and an overjoyed Ernest Mangnall addressed the crowd, with red and white favours thrown from the director's box. As the season ended the United secretary wasn't simply adhering to the matter at hand, but cast his eyes towards the months ahead and had already secured the signatures of the vast majority of his team for the new campaign. Goals had often been scored for fun, but those barren afternoons also sprang to mind, allowing the thoughts of improvement to filter through one's mind.

In J.H. Davies and J.E. Mangnall, Manchester United had undoubted men of ambition and having rescued Newton Heath from the jaws of obscurity, Davies in particular was determined to produce a club that was capable of meeting whatever challenges fell into their path and take Manchester United to whatever heights were attainable.

With the season barely confined to the record books, Mangnall pulled off what would be arguably seen as his one of his finest pieces of work for the club, the signing of a certain Billy Meredith. "Sensational Transfer – MEREDITH SIGNS FOR MANCHESTER UNITED" was the headline in the *Manchester Evening News* of Wednesday May 16th.

> *"As we indicated a fortnight ago Meredith, the well-known outside right has been signed by Manchester United. For reasons which are known to all followers of the game, Meredith did not take part in football last season, and quite a flutter was caused recently when it was announced that the Manchester City Executive had put him on the transfer list, placing the fee for his transfer at the large sum of £500.*
>
> *"Many clubs have been desirous of securing his services, but Meredith, for business and other reasons, was not desirous of leaving Manchester. The probabilities are that the player would have signed before now but for the fact that the findings in what has become known as the 'Meredith case' have not yet been made known.*
>
> *"Yesterday the famous winger had a long consultation with the Manchester United officials, which resulted in him signing the necessary forms,*

*but owing to various little details having to be fixed
up, we were not then in a position to announce
the fact. These have been complied with to-day,
and Meredith is now a member of the Manchester
United club. Although Meredith has been playing
football for over ten years, he has still few, if any,
superiors at outside right, and he should prove
a valuable acquisition to the Clayton club. The
outside right position last season was one of the
weak spots in the team, but next season it should
be exceptionally strong, for the names of Meredith
and Peddie look like forming a very strong wing."*

While the United support celebrated the signing of
the Welsh international, their City counterparts were up
in arms, annoyed at losing such a talented individual and
even more so at what they considered a give–away price,
as one shareholder pointed out that United, and indeed
a few other clubs, were more than willing to pay £1,500
for his signature.

Although a United player, Mangnall had no idea as to
where or when he could add the name of Meredith to his
team sheet, as the player was currently under suspension
by the Football League following an investigation into his
attempt to offer Alec Leake, captain of Aston Villa, £10
if he could persuade his team mates to let Manchester
City win a game between the clubs on April 29th 1905
as City chased the First Division title and more to the
point, a £100 bonus if they lifted the title or achieved the
same number of points as rivals Newcastle United. Found
guilty, Meredith was suspended from all football between
August 5th 1905 and April 30th 1906.

It would be January 1907 before anyone saw Billy
Meredith in the red shirt of Manchester United.

5: A FIRST DIVISION CLUB

FROM HIS SECRETARIAL DUTIES, to signing the likes of Yates and Buckley from Aston Villa, Ernest Mangnall had more on his mind as the sun shone brightly in the summer of 1906. Throughout his life he had been involved in some form of sporting activity, either competing or spectating. Away from the sporting arena, however, how much time he devoted to the ins and outs of everyday life is anyone's guess, but on Thursday July 12th he was married to Eliza Hobson at South Shore, Blackpool.

As you will have read earlier, his marriage certificate states that he was thirty-six, something that caused much confusion in relation to his early years, but such things are behind us now and no matter his real age, he was now manager of a First Division club, something that would more than likely take priority to life at his marital home - 13 Hill Street, Blackpool.

The Hill Street address was given as his residence on his marriage certificate and the newly-wed Manchester United secretary/manager did not have to concern himself with home improvements or the like, not that they would have been a distraction for more important work at Bank Street, Clayton. The usually quiet ground during the close season was a hive of activity with the noise of hammers and other necessary tools required for construction matters filling the air, mixing with the continuous smoke billowing from nearby chimneys.

There were many curious onlookers, some hoping to

spot the United secretary in the 'hat' he would wear in the close season, while his managerial duties were somewhat minimal, he would call them over and have them carry out some task or other with a shilling or so being handed over at the end of the day.

Extensive and much needed alterations were being carried out, an answer perhaps to the criticisms of those who thought Bank Street too Spartan and inadequate for the increasing number of people who wanted to spend their Saturday afternoon watching Mangnall's team in action. There had been talk of moving away from Clayton to a purpose built stadium but for the time being this remained United's home and J. H. Davies and his fellow directors were happy to spend to improve the ground.

A new stand, which could accommodate some 1,200 people, was the main body of work and this new construction would join the current 'reserved stand' and be carried across the Stuart Street corner of the ground to the large stand behind the Clayton goal. At the opposite end the embankment was being considerably extended and would in time hold 12,000 people who would have a view of the complete pitch.

The *Manchester Evening News* painted a narrative for its readers familiar with the ground:

> *"The seats inside the enclosure have been removed, and the hoardings carried four and a half feet forward along the entire length of the ground, and the nine feet thus gained will be utilised for standing room. To carry out this scheme the embankment has been lowered about two feet, and this alteration should, in particular, be welcomed by the occupants of the sixpenny side, as the change will mean that the touch line can be seen from any part of the large*

stand which runs along the chemical works.

"When the work is completed there will be a capital slope running from the stands on both sides of the ground to the hoardings. Holders of tickets for the reserved stand will pass behind the new structure, and gain admittance by means of a gangway near the referee and linesmen's rooms, this change doing away with the necessity of ticket holders having to fight their way through the crowd.

"The thick pillars on the best stand, which were a source of annoyance last season, are to be replaced by thin iron columns. The charge for tickets to this stand will be a guinea, and for the three remaining stands (one uncovered) will be 12s. 6d., whilst season tickets for the ground will be 12s. 6d. It is important that an early application should be made, as only a limited number will be issued. All the work will have been completed before the end of the season, and the ground should then be as good as any in the country. The playing pitch looks in splendid condition, being covered, with the exception of one small patch, with a splendid crop of grass, and in great contrast to the occasion when the memorable match with Aston Villa was played.

"Although Mr. Mangnall and the officials have been so busy in connection with the ground alterations, they have not neglected the playing strength of the team, but, like other football club managers, they find that really tip-top men are very difficult to obtain."

The improved environs at Clayton from pitch to top flight football, did not appease everyone as club President J. H. Davies received a letter from one irate supporter, which

he shared with his secretary/manager before passing to
the *Manchester Evening News*, the newspaper publishing it
on July 16th 1906:

> *"Sir, For several years I have been a season ticket
> holder in the 12s. 6d. part of the ground. During
> the past summer months I have organised a club
> to enable those interested in the United F.C. the
> opportunity of purchasing season tickets. To our
> surprise we find you have raised the price from
> 10s. 6d. to 12s. 6d., and the 12s. 6d. stand you
> have absorbed in the 21s. stand. The majority,
> if not all the members of the season ticket club,
> strongly object to buying season tickets, preferring
> to go to the popular side, and then to the best
> matches only. We do not consider it fair treatment
> after supporting the club for years watching Second
> League teams now there is an opportunity of being
> rewarded by First League football the prices are
> immediately advanced. Some years ago, you tried a
> 15s. stand, but it proved a failure, and at 12s. 6d.
> it was a success; so, we consider the original prices
> would pay the club better than the revised. I should
> be pleased if you would reconsider your decision,
> and if possible, let the prices be as last season,
> which would oblige many of the old supporters.
> Respectfully yours, S. STAFFORD. 29, North
> Road, Clayton; July 13, 1906."*

Two days later, yet another disgruntled supporter put
pen to paper:

> *"Sir, I was very pleased to read Mr. Stafford's
> letter in your valuable paper, and hope Mr. Davies
> and the directors of the club will give it careful*

consideration before they settle, finally, the price of season tickets. We are all aware the club has gained a higher position. Still, we ticket-holders consider we have paid first-class prices for inferior matches long enough, and think we are entitled to see better class at the old prices. I also wish to draw your attention to the fact that it is only ticket holders who are penalised for the club having gained a higher position. Spectators who go to the ground perhaps not more than two or three times a season are admitted at the old prices. I would like to ask Mr. Davies and the directors if they consider this fair treatment to their regular subscribers. I sympathise with Mr. Stafford, and hope he will achieve his points for the benefit of the old supporters. Yours, &C., ASTONISHED TICKET-HOLDER."

A reply, of sorts, appeared on July 19th, and although unaccredited to Ernest Mangnall, as the club secretary, it undoubtedly came from his pen. It read:

"The season tickets have been printed, and the question as to price is at an end, so far as the approaching season is concerned. When the prices were decided upon it was felt that it would be unfair to the Manchester City club if lower prices were charged at Clayton than was the case at Hyde Road, and it was only the true spirit of sportsmanship that actuated the directors in their decision. Only two League clubs in Lancashire charge less than the Manchester clubs, and when it is borne in mind that a ticket purchased for 8s. 6d. will enable the holder to witness a full programme of First League and Lancashire Combination

> *matches it is contended that there is very little cause*
> *for complaint."*

It was therefore a case of like it or lump it!

"Manchester United, who open the season at Bristol, have not captured many 'stars' during the close season, but with perhaps the exception of the centre-forward berth they should be able to turn out a strong side" remarked the *Lancashire Evening Post* on Saturday August 25th 1906. It hadn't been with the want of trying that Mangnall had failed to bring new faces to the club, as he had negotiated long and hard to sign Woolridge from Wolverhampton Wanderers and Morley from Grimsby Town without success.

Mangnall and his trainer, Fred Bacon, had been putting the players through their paces, even throwing in a game of cricket and they were fit and raring to go. Following a pre-season trial game, which allowed the supporters to cast an eye over their favourites, the players and officials boarded motor coaches and were taken to Mosley Hall, Cheadle, the residence of club president J. H. Davies where they were entertained and presented with solid gold medals to commemorate promotion into the First Division.

That J. E. Mangnall was the essential cog in the Manchester United machine was something not missed by anyone and the following appeared in the September 1st edition of the *Manchester Evening News*:

> *"For a team to be successful a good secretary is almost as necessary as a good centre-forward, and Manchester United are fortunate to possess a gentleman of the ability of Mr J. E. Mangnall. Prior to coming to Clayton, Mr Mangnall carried the Burnley club through a most serious crisis, and*

the honourable position the United now occupy is in a large measure due to his untiring efforts and enterprise. Only those who are acquainted with the inner working of the club can have any conception of the important duties he has been called upon to fulfill, and the fact that since Mr. Mangnall took office the period has been one of steady and continuous progress is sufficient testimony of his ability. Careful to a degree, Mr. Mangnall is yet one of the most keen and enthusiastic sportsmen connected with the game, and by his tact and unfailing courtesy he has done much for the club. His extensive knowledge of the game and its players has been placed unsparingly before his employers, and as a judge of players he has few superiors. Upon Mr. Mangnall fall the duties of secretary and manager, and during his three years' connection with the club he has proved himself a model official. The esteem in which he is held by the players was shown last Saturday when he received a most flattering reception on rising to receive one of the promotion medals."

Unlike at some clubs, the United players under Mangnall's charge were treated well, not simply with the odd extravagant meal in surroundings far removed from usual, but they would they would also be whisked off for four nights at a high class hotel such as St Vincent's Rock in Bristol that would be their headquarters prior to their opening match of the season before travelling up to Derby for the following fixture two days later.

It was somewhat strange that the new season would see the curtain rise with United coming face to face with Bristol City, the team they had pursued in the chase for the

Second Division championship during the course of the previous campaign and the same side that they had faced on the opening day of the 1904-05 season. Mangnall nor his players cared little as they had opened that previous season with a resounding 5-1 victory at Clayton and had drawn 1-1 in the return fixture at later in that season and it would continue in a similar vein this time around.

Manchester United's first season as a top flight club got off to the most promising start with a 2-1 victory at Bristol, before a point was secured in a 2-2 draw at Derby. Even a point in the first home fixture, a 0-0 draw against Notts County, would have been welcomed by many as the club slowly found their feet in their new surroundings. The second victory of the season, 2-0 at Sheffield United, came on September 15th and was followed a week later by the first defeat, 2-1 against Bolton Wanderers at Clayton and by the end of October they had played ten, won four, drawn four and lost two. Their twelve points, although four behind leaders Everton, kept them well in touch with the leading pack.

Despite what could be regarded as a favourable start, Mangnall wasn't entirely happy and was soon off to Ireland in the search for new players, hoping to obtain the signature of Howard Sloan of Dublin Bohemian, but he preferred to remain on home soil, so the journey proved a waste of time. Unperturbed he was soon packing his overnight bag once again, this time heading for Scotland, a more fruitful destination for Manchester United officials in years gone by. Heading to Ayrshire he signed Arthur Young from Hurlford, a twenty-year-old winger with a good reputation. Straight into the first team he went, but after just two appearances he was to become a permanent member of the United reserve side. So it was back on the road for the United secretary and in mid-November he could once again be found in the land of heather and haggis and beneath the towering castle in Edinburgh. *"Have just signed Alex Menzies, Heart of Midlothian and Scottish International centre-forward. – Mangnall"* read the telegram that winged its way back to Manchester on November 14th and a problem position within the Clayton ranks had been solved, for the meantime at least. An outside-right was now considered a priority, with some even suggesting that Mangnall should play Meredith and worry about the wrath of the Football League later. That problem position was filled soon after the arrival of Menzies when William Berry was signed from Tottenham Hotspur, although it was his previous club, Sunderland, who received the £40 transfer fee as Spurs were still a Southern League team. Both players made their league bows in a 5-2 defeat at Sheffield Wednesday, the only plus point of the ninety minutes being Menzies scoring on his debut.

Many in the game were of the opinion that money was no object to Manchester United and Mangnall had a bottomless purse to work with, but such suggestions were rebuffed in early November during the United secretary's pursuit of Fred Rouse of Stoke City, when it transpired that a £750 transfer fee stood in the way. A forward of great ability, his appearance in the red shirt might have been of great benefit to United, but the ghost of Billy Meredith was still haunting Clayton, and Rouse, who was to join Everton, may well have found himself a bit part player and not all were happy to play the role of understudy to the great Welshman.

November 1906 brought the realities of First Division football home to everyone at Clayton with only one victory [1-0 at home to Woolwich Arsenal] from four games. Defeats at Everton [3-0], Sheffield Wednesday [5-2] and a home defeat to Bury [4-2] them into the lower half of the table, seven points equidistant between table-toppers Arsenal and basement-dwellers Middlesbrough.

A change of month, never mind starting elevens, failed to produce a change in fortune as the first Saturday in December saw United travel across Manchester to Hyde Road, where second-bottom City inflicted a resounding 3-0 defeat in front of a highly charged and passionate forty odd thousand spectators. Some of the £1,100 in gate takings, however, would have to have been spent on repairs as City officials had ordered the gates to be closed at two o'clock with thousands still outside and some of the entrances were broken down by those determined to see the game.

On the field, at least, December proved as fruitless as November, with only one victory, 3-1 against Middlesbrough, and if you couldn't defeat the bottom club what hope did you have? Points, thankfully, were secured from goalless draws against Liverpool and Bristol City, while along with that defeat to City, Preston North End, Newcastle United and Aston Villa took both points. But amid those dark, dismal afternoons at Clayton and elsewhere there was soon to be a glow of light around that Mancunian district and not from Christmas trees or other festive decorations.

Ernest Mangnall, like an excited child, was counting down those December days, but not for the awaited arrival of Father Christmas. Even good old Santa Claus could not bring him what he had on his wish list. Although United reportedly couldn't agree on a transfer fee for the recently sought after Rouse, Mangnall's request to his benefactor, and club president, J. H. Davies to take a squad of thirteen players to Blackpool's Norbreck Hall for the best part of December was given the green light, as was the go-ahead to increase the playing staff, not to mention wage bill, by not one, but four individuals.

The reason for Mangnall's glee was the anticipated fire-sale of players at Hyde Road following an FA enquiry that had suspended or banned seventeen current and former City players due to having received illegal payments and these bans would all end on New Years Day 1907. The Hyde Road club had been gutted from top to bottom and as top class talent hit the open market Mangnall recognised that as their closest neighbours United effectively had first dibs. Canny Ernest was keen to add three more City players to his squad following the acquisition of Meredith: left-back Herbert Burgess and forwards Sandy Turnbull and Jimmy Bannister. Edmondson had been another of interest but he joined Bolton Wanderers.

The subterfuge required to pull off the heist of the century was breathtaking and illustrates Ernest Mangnall's unique talents. Burgess was first to put pen to paper, much to the annoyance of Glasgow Celtic and Everton, both clubs having been of the opinion that the defender was heading their way. Besides those two clubs Newcastle United, Leeds City, Bolton Wanderers and Bradford had all expressed an interest. Newcastle, Celtic and Bolton arrived at Hyde Road with cheque books in hand on Monday December 3rd, but they were two days too late as Mangnall had already presented City with a cheque signed by J. H. Davies and whisked Burgess off to an unknown address in central Manchester until the heat died down.

Heat there certainly was, as City had apparently agreed to sell him to Everton, with the Merseyside club having shown an interest in the player as far back as September, stating that they held a document to that effect, with their club minute books from that time confirming that a fee of £600 had been offered for the player. But no matter their moans and complaints, Herbert Burgess was now a Manchester United player, even if a couple of City directors informed the *Manchester Courier* differently. A brief and to the point article in the *Manchester Evening News* of Thursday December 6th confirmed that City had indeed lost Burgess, Turnbull and Bannister to their local rivals:

> *"Following upon an announcement yesterday with regard to the transfer of Burgess to Manchester United, we are officially informed this afternoon by Mr. Magnall [sic], the secretary of the United Club, that everything is in order with regard to the transfer of that player and Turnbull and Bannister. Forms have been signed by all three players, and their transfers are now complete. The forms have been sent to the Football Association and the League for registration, and the whole business is now settled."*

The Burgess fiasco rumbled on for a month. If the proposed transfer between City and Everton had not also involved Percy Hill moving from Merseyside to Manchester then things would have been rather simple, as it was (according to the *Manchester Evening News*): –

> *"Everton agreed to transfer Hill to Manchester City in exchange for Burgess or £600. Having failed to secure Burgess, they will receive £600 from the City club who will have to pay to the League, for the benefit of charities, everything*

above £600 received from Manchester United for Burgess. Thus, if United pay City £750 there will £150, less the costs of the meeting, for division. Rumour has it that Manchester United are paying £1,000 and if that be correct, charities will benefit by nearly £400."

There was no mention of wrongdoing by Mangnall or anyone connected with United.

New Year's Day was a red letter day for Mangnall, Davies and United followers. The midnight chimes saw glasses raised in the hope that 1907 would be a prosperous one for family and friends alike, while the red half of the city had a special toast for their football club and its new dawn.

Having been in training at the sports ground adjacent to the Belle Vue Zoological Gardens, the recently acquired City contingent were as fit as they could be considering the circumstances and were raring to go and Mangnall had no hesitation in including the quartet of Meredith, Turnbull, Bannister and Burgess in his team to meet Aston Villa at Clayton.

"It is very questionable whether any previous game in Manchester has aroused more interest than the one at Clayton yesterday" remarked the *Manchester Evening News* the following day, adding:

> *"It was to be regretted that owing to the Bank-street end of the ground getting blocked so many were unable to gain admission. As it was over 40,000 people witnessed the game, and they were rewarded by seeing a very fine game indeed. The "gate" and the game were certainly remarkable considering the conditions, as rain fell heavily throughout, and the playing portion was one huge heap of mud. Chief*

interest of course centred in the reappearance of Meredith, Burgess, Turnbull, and Bannister, and in the play of the first mentioned in particular.

The Welshman early on demonstrated that he still retained his remarkable form and there were some who contended that he never played a better game. He certainly played wonderful football throughout, although at times he was somewhat unfairly treated, and it was through a supreme effort of his that Turnbull scored the goal which won the game for Manchester. Bannister looks like making him a good partner and Duckworth supported the wing in splendid fashion. Turnbull is rather bulky, but he played his part well. Wall was to some extent neglected, and the halves would do well to distribute the play evenly. Burgess showed a falling off in the second half, but the great little back is sure to improve upon yesterday's display. The Villa gave a great exhibition, and on the run of the play were the better side, but they could not take advantage of the openings that came. They found Moger plenty of work as it was, but the ex-Southampton man was in brilliant form."

So had Mangnall got his 'perfect team' at last? There was no denying the strength in depth that he now had at his disposal, although he was to reduce the Mangnall United wage bill towards the end of January, selling Peddie, Wombwell and Yates to Heart of Midlothian, and surely the three blank goals for column that had materialised over the course of the final three fixtures of 1906 were a thing of the past. Sadly not, as four days later the new-look United struggled at second-bottom Notts County, the tenth club to visit Trent Bridge that season and the first to leave defeated. Defeat was also to come in the F.A. Cup, 2-1 against Portsmouth in a replay following a 2-2 draw, but in the league they started to gel and it was Sandy Turnbull who quickly became the new hero of Clayton, and perhaps saviour of Mangnall, scoring once in a 2-1 victory over Sheffield United and the only goal in a 1-0 victory over Bolton Wanderers. With Turnbull missing through injury and Bannister also side-lined for the first fixture in February away at Newcastle United, the team were soundly beaten 5-0, although it was to prove something of a one-off, as the following Saturday, still without the same duo, Stoke City were beaten 4-1, with Meredith claiming his first United goal. A week later he notched a double, helping to see off Blackburn Rovers in a 4-2 victory.

In training Mangnall would cajole and encourage his players as he worked to bring the best out of them, but he was to take his vocal attributes to a different level if a letter to the *Athletic News* in early February was to be believed. Under the heading of "Objectionable Practice" the *Athletic News* correspondent John Lewis wrote:

> *"Another Lancashire enthusiast sends me a cutting from a newspaper stating that at a match in which Manchester United were concerned the secretary of that club stood behind the goal all through the second half of the game, advising and encouraging his goalkeeper. He adds: 'You were at the Bolton Wanderers v. Manchester United match on the 26th last month, where there was a man on the stand side walking up and down with Meredith. Is this the usual practice with United?' I certainly did attend the match referred to, but I confess I did not notice anyone walking or running alongside*

*the right winger. I am surprised to hear it was so,
and cannot conceive what good he could imagine
he was doing. On the other hand, his presence was
decidedly objectionable, for what one man did others
might feel compelled to imitate. Such practice, if
practice it is, should be prohibited by the referee as
calculated to bring about trouble and disorder. But
the home club would have been within their rights
in ordering the man leave the ground. Whether he
was an official of the visiting club or not, he had
no right to be there. And on his own ground the
presence of an official advising players is equally
objectionable, and if the referee did not notice it the
visiting players might very properly protest.'"*

Needless to say the following week there was further
correspondence into the matter, with a much-aggrieved
J. E. Mangnall given his right to reply. John Lewis wrote:

*"I am not surprised to get a letter from Mr.
Mangnall indignantly contradicting the implication
that he had acted 'contrary to any rule of the
F.A. or my conscience as a sportsman.' The first
incident, he says, occurred two seasons ago, when
he had to stand with scores of others behind the
goal because that was the only place from which
view of the play could got. As to the other, he does
not think there is a word truth in it - certainly
none of his people remember anything of the sort.
It will be remembered, that I said last week that,
although I was at the Bolton match, I never saw
the "running gentleman" described. I imputed no
unsportsmanlike conduct to Mr. Mangnall, but,
replying to the specific question put to me, I said*

*that if such a thing did happen, the referee and the
other club would be entitled to resent it."*

There was never any possibility of United getting
anywhere near the First Division title as the 1906-07
season progressed with a 3-0 victory against Preston
North End at the end of February that saw them occupy a
respectable eighth place eleven points behind leaders and
eventual champions Newcastle United and a comfortable
fifteen above bottom club Stoke City. The remaining two
months of the season saw United win five, lose two and
draw two and gave time for Mangnall to run the rule over
his players, decide if there were any positions that required
strengthening, while looking at opposition players that he
considered better who might add an extra dimension to
his team.

He certainly didn't waste his time as no sooner had
the season drawn to a close with United finishing in a
comfortable eighth, than he signed Bolton goalkeeper
Herbert Bloomfield, and Barnsley full back George
Stacey. The latter was perhaps an essential commodity, as
Mangnall had lost Tommy Blackstock in early April in
tragic circumstances. With ten minutes of a reserve team
fixture against St Helens at Clayton on April 8th played
Blackstock fell to the ground with play at the opposite
end of the pitch. Having noticed the player fall backwards,
the referee's attention was caught, the game stopped and
Mangnall and two trainers ran onto the pitch. Blackstock
was carried from the field and a doctor sent for, but before
the doctor arrived the player had died.

Mangnall, having overseen Blackstock's body being
taken to the Mill Street Mortuary, told a waiting member
of the press that the player had been about thirty yards
from any other player when he fell and that the last thing

he did in the game was to head the ball out of play. The ground was light, and the ball did not weigh any more than sixteen or seventeen ounces, so that there appeared to be no question of a blow having caused death. He added that he thought the player must have fallen in a fit.

The dark cloud of Blackstock's death hovered above Clayton for some time and three days after the tragic accident his coffin was conveyed to Victoria Station from the mortuary in an open car, where some of his team mates acted as pall-bearers, while Mangnall, Stafford and the remainders players and trainers walked solemnly behind, as a number of supporters looked on. His body was carried onto a train on its first leg of a journey north to Kirkcaldy for burial.

With the season over any crumb of football news was eagerly grasped by supporters and Mangnall certainly gave Clayton die-hards food for thought as April drew to a close. Having had to delay the re-signing of his current squad due to the birth of his son, James Ernest, Mangnall informed the *Manchester Evening News* that "things were proceeding very satisfactorily", whilst also denying a rumour in circulation that the club had secured a new ground adjoining the Manchester Racecourse, which was actually in Salford, although he did give food for thought by adding, *"but it is the intention of the directorate to provide a suitable home for the club as soon as circumstances permit. Where this will be, however, has not yet been settled."*

6: CHAMPIONS

THE CLOSE SEASON saw Mangnall as busy as ever, whether he found time for strolls along the seafront at Blackpool with his wife and pushing the pram of his young son is up for debate, but I doubt if it was a regular routine. Perhaps when the dust settled on the season past and he got the business of re-signing and bringing new players in out of the way, then some quality leisure time may well have been in order. Yet May certainly kept him busy in and around Clayton. He oversaw the transfers of Vince Hayes to Brentford and Robert Bonthron to Sunderland, while adding Jimmy Turnbull, and lesser-known names such as McLarney, a full-back from Norwich City, Routledge, a centre-forward from Hooley Hill, Whiteside from Irvine and Mills of Willenhall, another centre-forward, to the playing staff. Turnbull, no relation to his namesake Sandy, arrived from Leyton and although the unknowns in Routledge and Mills had scored twenty-six and twenty goals respectively for their clubs in the past season, neither would have the opportunity to deliver similar totals in the Football League, nevertheless Turnbull would prove to be yet another excellent signing, as the former Preston North End and Glasgow Rangers player was considered to be the best centre-forward in the south of England.

Having taken the jump from the Second Division to First in his stride, Mangnall had assembled a team which, on paper at least, looked set to challenge for honours. The Manchester City 'miscreants' had seen much of the rust from their prolonged inactivity disappear over those final four months of the season and now, with a full pre-season training under their belt, everyone at Clayton was prepared for the campaign ahead. "The prospects of Manchester United are excellent" proclaimed the *Sporting Life*.

It was with bated breath that Mangnall watched United's first competitive encounter as his players, or at least some of them, took on Bolton Wanderers in a game of 'Pushball' at Bolton's Royal Show'. Although nothing more than an added spectacle to the day's events, the game, where you had to push the five to six foot high inflated ball between the goal posts, was taken seriously by all involved. The scoring was rather complicated, it was after all an American game, with a point each time the ball went behind the posts by the attackers, two when it was sent behind by the defenders and four if it went between the posts. Two games were played, with both ending in draws 2-2 and 4-4.

The 1907-08 season opened with an away fixture at Aston Villa on Bank Holiday Monday September 2nd and the training, pushball, not to mention a cricket match against neighbours City and an evening as guests of club president J. H. Davies had the players in tiptop condition, with their opponents swept aside, having no answer to United's free-flowing football. Goals from Bannister, Wall and a Meredith double gave United a 4-1 victory and the ideal start to the season.

"Manchester United In Brilliant Form" shouted the local *Evening News*, adding that it was considered *"one of the best performances since the club was founded"* while the *London Daily News* echoed "Sensational Victory Of Manchester United At Aston", with their man at the match being of the opinion that *"The United opened in most business like fashion, and created an excellent impression by their smart combination and clever individual work."*

When Liverpool arrived in Clayton four more goals were scored, on this occasion without reply, Sandy Turnbull outdoing Meredith's double in the season opener with a hat-trick with George Wall adding the other. Middlesbrough followed Liverpool to Manchester two days later but, like the Merseysiders, were to find little in the way of generosity as United made it three out of three with a 2-1 victory. Sandy Turnbull netting both.

"Mr Mangnall has worked matters up to a high state of efficiency at Clayton, and Mr. John Bentley told me they would have a very fine team this season" wrote 'Throstle' of the *Daily Mirror* following that hat-trick of early season victories. He continued:

> *"And so they have. Willie Meredith is still wonderful, and I can guarantee left full backs one of their hardest times of the season when they meet Meredith, Bannister, and Duckworth. The last-named is the most improved half-back of the year. On the other wing young Sandy Turnbull is absolutely thrilling in front of goal, and Scotland need look nowhere else for her inside left if the youngster keeps in his present form."*

It wasn't, however, going to be all plain sailing, as the return fixture against Middlesbrough five days later brought the first reversal of the season in a 2-1 defeat. It was a disappointment, but United still looked down on their First Division rivals, albeit on goal average, with Middlesbrough and Bury also sitting on six points.

Defeat in the north-east was to prove little more than

an unwanted itch, as it was immediately back on the winning trail, leaving all and sundry in their wake, with goals coming from all angles and not just from man of the moment Sandy Turnbull and it would be the end of November before defeat was tasted again.

It was obviously the United players who achieved the on-field results, with the press voicing their approval and praise of Messrs Turnbull, Meredith and co., but the part played by J. E. Mangnall was never forgotten. In the 'Football Comments' column of the *Sporting Chronicle* of Wednesday October 16th 1907 could be found: "In Ernest Mangnall the United have a shrewd secretary". The article lauded United's all-round ability *"proved by their splendid goal record; 27-7 – almost an average of 4-1 in their favour"* adding, *"Like Angoulaffre, the giant of Jerusalem, who had the power of thirty men – Manchester United are strong everywhere, and live up to their name."*

United's early season form, although viewed with some jealousy around the country, was also acknowledged by the press in other areas of the country. 'Manchester United's Greatness' was a heading from the *Leeds Mercury* towards the end of October, their correspondent writing after the 5-1 victory against Blackburn Rovers:

> *"There is no doubt that Manchester United are the most wonderful team of the season. Their forwards are remarkably clever in finding the net, as a goal average of nearly four a match suggests; while their defence also stands out as superior to that of any other club in the First League. Blackburn Rovers are reckoned a warm side at home, and it was thus a startling performance for the United to win five goals to one. This is not the Manchester United we saw at Leeds and Bradford a couple of years*

ago. Manchester United's big victory is all the more amazing from the fact that the Rovers had not previously lost either a point or a goal at Ewood Park this season."

That 5-1 victory at Blackburn [Sandy Turnbull notching three and Jimmy Turnbull the other two], was clearly a sign of intent from Mangnall's men in their challenge for the championship and their performances were being noted far and wide. The *Staffordshire Sentinel* commented:

"The strong United of Manchester continued their victorious career last Saturday by recording a sensational win of five goals to one at Blackburn. Prior to this occasion the Rovers had neither lost a point nor a goal at Ewood Park, but they were altogether outclassed by the brilliant Clayton men, and were as far behind as the score indicates. For the second time this season Sandy Turnbull got the hat trick, and he appears to be about as dangerous in front of goal just now as anyone playing football. The side is a great one, and while every position is filled as well as it could be, there is a perfect understanding among the men. There are some people around and about Cottonopolis who predict a career for the United like unto that of Preston North End in the old days, but we cannot overlook the fact that the opposition of to-day is infinitely stronger, in comparison, than it was then. Still, should the club we once knew as Newton Heath practically carry all before them, as their present form suggests, their work will, by reason of this fact, be all the more creditable."

Seven days prior to that 5-1 trouncing of Blackburn Rovers, United had bettered that score line at St James's Park, Newcastle when the Turnbulls, along with Charlie Roberts, Billy Meredith and two from George Wall, demolished the reigning First Division champions 6-1. Following that defeat against Middlesbrough, as well as those high-scoring ninety minutes against Blackburn and Newcastle, Sheffield United were beaten 2-1 at Clayton [Sandy Turnbull notching both], Chelsea 4-1 at Stamford Bridge [Meredith 2, Bannister and Sandy Turnbull], Nottingham Forest 4-0 at Clayton [Bannister, Jimmy Turnbull, Meredith and an own goal] and Bolton Wanderers 2-1 also at Clayton [Sandy and Jimmy Turnbull].

There was little doubt as to who led the First Division at the end of October. United were five points clear of Sheffield Wednesday and six in front of Manchester City and Everton. Ernest Mangnall was a proud and happy man, but was he also supplementing his Manchester United salary, with additional payments in the form of sponsorship or advertising?

Newspapers ranging from the *Sussex Agricultural Express* to the *Athletic News* saw him endorsing Alec Watson's Famous League Football, in adverts which contained a quote from the United secretary/manager – "Your 'League' ball gave every satisfaction", while Mr Watson's Oxford Street business also offered everything from 'flannelette shirts', [boys 15/6, Men's 19/- a dozen, over 1,000 dozen in stock and over fifty colour designs], 'knickers' [special price for dozens] to 'goal nets' [27/-, 34/- and 40/- per set complete]. His name was also linked with Oxo – 'Manchester United On Oxo' – "Our players speak very highly of Oxo, and find it very beneficial during an arduous season" – J. E. Mangnall, Secretary, Manchester United.' Whether or not there was a nice little earner here and there, it certainly kept him and the club in the public eye.

Prior to the 2-1 victory over Bolton Wanderers at Clayton an article appeared in the *Farringdon Advertiser and Vale of the White* "specially written by 'Tam'", under the heading of 'The Secret Of The Success Of Manchester United'. There wasn't one really. United simply won games by scoring more goals than their opponents with a team of exciting individuals put together by a knowledgeable manager, but it was how that manager had put things together that 'Tam' focused on. Within his article, he wrote:

> *"I know Turnbull [Jimmy] who leads Manchester United's attacking line, and he is just the sort of man I should expect to succeed at this forcing game. Now Turnbull met with but moderate success as a centre-forward while he was with Leyton – a Southern League club. It was hardly his fault. He was ready to go through the opposition with his head up; but the men on either side of him were not able to render support. Manchester United, however, knew their man tolerably well. He was just the kind of player they wanted, for they knew their inside man and wingers too. Manchester United, I am told, play the forcing game to perfection. They converge on the goal; they have found the net not once, but three or four times in recent matches. They are top of the table and they may win the championship. The forcing game is the secret of their success."*

November was more or less identical to October, if you forget the 2-0 defeat at Owlerton against Sheffield Wednesday on the last day of the month, with victories against Birmingham City 4-3 at St Andrews [Meredith 2, J. Turnbull and Wall], Everton 4-3 at Clayton [Wall 2, Meredith and Roberts], Sunderland 2-1 at Roker Park [Sandy Turnbull 2] and Woolwich Arsenal 4-2 at Clayton [Sandy Turnbull 4]. Despite the reversal in Sheffield, United stood firm at the top, four points ahead of the Wednesday, but a massive nine points ahead of third placed Newcastle United.

There was now talk of Mangnall's men breaking records. At present, Newcastle United and Liverpool tied for the largest total of points with fifty-one. United already had twenty-eight from fifteen fixtures so only required twenty-five from twenty-three matches. No team since 1899 had held a four-point lead after the opening three months of the season, while their forty-eight goals in those first three months was also a total unequalled by any club since 1899. A sobering thought however was that for the past ten years the club leading at the beginning of December had failed to lift the championship crown come April.

At this time it appeared that Manchester United had no worries whatsoever, they were on the crest of a wave, buoyant as regards to their progress and although their Bank Street ground may have looked a little dismal, there was a ray of sunshine about the place. So much so that no-one, including the United secretary/manager, noticed the dark cloud beginning to appear over the Manchester chimney tops.

Football had changed immensely in recent years and was continuing to do so at a steady rate of knots. The transfer system had been adjusted so that no club could approach a player without the permission of the club that held his registration. However, according to one reporter of the time – *"the players were simply a shuttlecock, knocked to and fro between the parties who were contending for possession of his person."* Adding, *"By being outspoken in these days many a player has been deprived of his means of living owing to the arbitrary action of the clubs negotiating for his services, putting a prohibitive price upon his head."* It was now that the players decided that enough was enough.

There had been a Players Union way back in February 1898, but this was relatively short lived and had folded in 1901. Little, however, had changed, as players were seen by many clubs as nothing more than a commodity, like a horse pulling a cart being replaced when it became too old and a younger one brought in their stead.

It is perhaps no coincidence that the seeds for such an organisation were sown among the suspended Manchester City players who soon became Manchester United players – Messrs Turnbull, Bannister, Burgess and in particular Billy Meredith. The ban from playing the game they loved, and the means that provided them with their livelihood, would have been hard to take, but it gave Meredith time to think. He may well have cast his thoughts back a few years when two City players had died in tragic circumstances - Di Jones having cut his leg during a pre-season trial game before dying from blood poisoning and lock-jaw and Jimmy Ross, one of the founding members of the original Players' Union, who died soon after retiring from the game due to ill-health - both families were left more or less penniless. He could also have been disillusioned and disgruntled with the authorities, although he was to deny that his idea of forming a Union was not in defiance or to cause annoyance to the Football Association. Perhaps in the knowledge of what might befall him if the hierarchy thought otherwise.

November 1907 found Meredith on his soapbox – *"We are bought and sold like sheep or cattle, and that is not a nice thing to reflect on"* he proclaimed, adding that it was not uncommon for a club to get rid of a player if that individual had a benefit payment due. By the end of the month, he had *"issued circulars to the captains of all the First Division clubs in the north of England, Lancashire, Yorkshire and the Midlands"*, inviting them to a meeting in Manchester the following week.

Many of the players were already members of the Association Football Players' and Trainers Union, but having held talks away from Clayton with Charlie Roberts, other team mates and players from other clubs, it was decided that now was the time to stand up and be counted.

Whether or not Ernest Mangnall had any inclination as to what his players were up, or had perhaps been sounded out, to is anyone's guess, but there is little doubt that he would have been supportive of their cause, if not immediately, certainly through time, perhaps more so when his benefactor and United Chairman J. H. Davies who became the Union's vice-president.

Meredith, Roberts and co. held their first official meeting in United director Harry Stafford's pub, The Imperial Hotel on London Road, Manchester on December 2nd. Presided over by Meredith, representatives from Preston North End, Sunderland, Newcastle United, Bury, Oldham Athletic, West Bromwich Albion, Sheffield United and Bradford Park Avenue, along with all the

City and United players reportedly present and it was unanimously agreed to form a union, with an un-named sub-committee formed. Letters of support also came from the captains of Nottingham Forest, Notts County, Aston Villa, Sheffield Wednesday, Everton, Stoke City, Derby County and Leeds City. I mention that all the City players were 'reportedly' present, as one paper does not name them as being amongst the attendees, while that paper states that Liverpool had representatives present, while another states that the only clubs of note that didn't respond were Bolton Wanderers, Middlesbrough and Liverpool. Another paper mentions that Birmingham City were another club who had not replied to the letter.

The formation of the Union put Mangnall in a difficult position. Regardless of his sympathies, he was involved in every aspect of the day to day running of Manchester United and would see his players on a daily basis and although the majority of the initial work to get the union off the ground was carried out by Herbert Broomfield, who had played for both Manchester clubs, the United contingent were now at the forefront of the movement and in United's star player William Meredith they had a charismatic and outspoken opponent of the status quo within professional football.

It was against this background that a possibly distracted Manchester United dropped more points in two drawn fixtures that December against Notts County 1-1 [Meredith] at Trent Bridge and Preston North End 0-0 at Deepdale, although three home victories - 2-1 [Wall 2] against Bristol City, 3-1 [Sandy Turnbull 2 and Wall] against neighbours City and 2-1 [Meredith and Jimmy Turnbull] against Bury, saw them maintain a more than comfortable nine-point advantage over second placed

Newcastle United. The latter's game in hand mattered little. If there was to be a downside, it came in the Manchester 'derby' where, despite the tense rivalry, Sandy Turnbull was sent off for nothing more than a flick of his hand across the neck of Dorsett. The *Manchester Evening News* commented: *"Unless it was that the City forward was so shocked at receiving anything in the nature of a blow from his friend it is difficult to account for the tragic manner in which he reeled and fell"*.

Turnbull's dismissal cast a shadow over the derby victory, not in so much the action of the current United talisman, but from an after-match incident which led to an appearance by the United management in front of the F.A. following a letter of complaint from the match official in which the referee, Mr T.P. Campbell of Blackburn, complained that at the end of the game he entered the United office to receive his match fee and was subjected to insults from two people and that Mr J. J. Bentley, vice-president of the F.A., president of the Football League and a United director, did nothing to protect him from the comments directed towards him.

> *"Dear Sir, I would like to ask whether it is fair and reasonable that officials, upon entering an office of a club crowded with excited partisans to draw their fees, should be insulted and sneered at as were the two linesmen and myself on Saturday last at the United ground? This was done in the presence of a vice-president of the Football Association.*
>
> *"I refer to Mr. J. J. Bentley, who allowed these remarks to be made without remonstrating with the man who made them, notwithstanding my protests. Such conduct towards the servants the Football Association regrettable. Yours truly, T. P. Campbell."*

Campbell's referee's report read:

"I have to report sending off the field play of S. Turnbull, of the United Club, in the match between the above teams played on Saturday last. In the first half I had occasion to warn and then caution Turnbull upon his conduct, and in second half he struck Dorsett, of Manchester City, in the face with the back hand. I at once ordered him off. The blow was certainly a mild one, and undoubtedly Turnbull received provocation from the attitude Dorsett took up; but in the face of the previous caution, I had no option.

"I regret that for some little time after this several of the players on both sides appeared to lose their heads and indulged in childish and reprehensible tactics that, to say the least of it, were anything but creditable to them, and yet not of sufficient character to enable me to carry out greater powers invested in me. Yours sincerely, T. P. Campbell."

At the subsequent hearing it was revealed that the remarks made in Mangnall's office had come from a Mr. Walter Brearley, who was not present at the hearing, but evidence was heard from the referee and his linesmen, along with that of Mangnall and Bentley. Turnbull was suspended for a fortnight, while the resulting hearing saw no action taken against United, although it was stated that in future all clubs must give the match officials their fees in the changing areas.

Eleven days into the new year, following a 1-0 New Years Day victory over Bury thanks to a George Wall goal, the F.A. Cup programme got underway when Blackpool visited Clayton. To date the competition had proved fruitless to Mangnall, but having established United as a force to be reckoned with, no team held any fear and the competition was a nice distraction from the First Division, although lifting the championship crown was most definitely the main priority.

Blackpool were defeated 3-1 but Mangnall was forced into making a trio of changes for the trip to Sheffield United as he would be without Duckworth, Roberts and the suspended Sandy Turnbull, which resulted in a first defeat since the end of November, ironically at Blades' neighbours Wednesday.

It was a blip, nothing more, as it was back to winning ways seven days later with a Jimmy Turnbull goal enough to defeat Chelsea at Clayton. The Londoners were to return north the following Saturday, this time on cup business and once again a Turnbull goal, this time from Sandy, was enough to secure a place in round three.

Mid-February brought excitement within the ranks of the also-rans of the First Division, as United dropped points on consecutive Saturdays for the first time that season, drawing 1-1 with Newcastle United and losing 2-1 to Blackburn Rovers, both at Clayton. Could this be the start of a downward spiral for Mangnall's team, with the opportunity arising to make up some of the distance that had transpired over the course of the previous weeks and months?

Groans, however, were soon to echo around the division as United returned to winning ways again thanks to a Sandy Turnbull goal against Birmingham City in what was a third consecutive home fixture. Their lead remained impressive, eight points in front of Newcastle United, who had a game in hand, and nine in front of third placed Sheffield Wednesday. There were also talk of a cup and league double, as the F. A. Cup fourth round tie at Aston Villa resulted in a 2-0 victory.

March 1908 proved a strange month in the Manchester United calendar, as it not only brought an end to any interest that they had in the F. A. Cup when they lost 2-1 at Fulham, but it also produced another hiccup on the First Division front, with a 1-0 reversal at Woolwich Arsenal and a surprising 7-4 defeat at Liverpool within a four-day period.

Defeat at Craven Cottage would have come as a shock to Mangnall who had taken a squad of fifteen players south to Bedford prior to the match. *"The week has been quietly spent"* reported the United manager, *"the training work consisting of ball practise, sprinting and walking. The men are so fit after their hard season that they require training with care and we are not overdoing it. The week has been fine and the players have enjoyed their stay. We shall return to Bedford on Saturday night and travel on to Manchester on Sunday."* Few clubs could stretch to the luxury of a week away and it was of little wonder that envious glances continued to be made towards the club in regards to both their off and on field actions but a 2-1 defeat to a team freshly promoted to Football League Division Two sent shock-waves through the game.

Matters appeared to return to normality a week later when goals from Bell, Berry and Wall were enough to sink Sunderland at Clayton. It was becoming clear that without Sandy Turnbull United were a completely different team and now Mangnall came in for criticism in some areas for playing Berry instead of Sandy's namesake Jimmy at Plumstead, a fault he corrected against Liverpool. United made four changes to the side that had lost at Arsenal, but with the resources at hand Mangnall should have been able to call on adequate replacements, although to be fair, there was a huge gulf of difference between playing in the Lancashire Combination and the First Division but with Burgess, Bell and Sandy Turnbull all missing, United struggled and 'Anfield Sensation' was the headline of the day as United went down 7-4.

The result was a second shock to the system of everyone involved with the club that month and reduced the lead at the top of the First Division to five points, although United had two games in hand over their nearest rivals Newcastle United. Thankfully things got back on track three days later with a 4-1 victory over third place Sheffield Wednesday.

Sensing a need for some vital surgery and despite recently having challenged on two fronts, Mangnall looked towards improvement, attempting to construct a team as near to international class as possible, however, it still came as something of surprise to the majority when news filtered through on March 23rd that he had signed Harold Halse from Southern League Southend United for a reported maximum fee of £300. Numerous clubs in both England and Scotland had been interested in the Leytonstone-born forward but once more Mangnall had stealthily made his move and secured the players signature before other clubs realised that United were interested.

The *Manchester Courier* described Halse as, "a remarkable player" and detailed his scoring feats; he had scored some 125 goals the previous season, heading the list of professional footballers, while twelve months previously he had notched up "the remarkable figure of 229". This season to date he had amassed eighty-two. In the five games leading up to his transfer alone, he had scored fourteen. No wonder Mangnall had moved quickly.

With the arrival of a proverbial goal machine, albeit in the Southern League, coupled with the likes of Sandy Turnbull, Billy Meredith and George Wall, the Manchester United goals for total should have been in for a healthy increase. Halse scored on his debut, the 4-1 victory over Wednesday, but was overshadowed by two goal George Wall, although he found the net two games later in a 3-1 victory against Everton. Sandwiched in between was a 1-1 draw with Bristol City where Wall made it five goals in three games outdoing the new arrival.

That 3-1 victory at Goodison left United ten points clear of Newcastle United, who lost 5-2 against Aston Villa, with two games in hand and was enough to finally confirm that the championship crown would be seen at Clayton, as even if Newcastle won all their remaining four games they would still be two points short of United's total.

It was perhaps just as well that United had put themselves in an unassailable position, as Notts County arrived at Clayton on the afternoon of April 11th and left at tea-time with a 1-0 victory, having stunned the 20,000 present. It was a case of the away team being in desperate need of the points as defeat would have left them staring at relegation.

Had Mangnall's men taken their eye off the ball having led the First Division for so long and having the League championship trophy in the bag? Many, including some of their own supporters thought they had, but even they were numbed six days later when Notts County's near neighbours Nottingham Forest also defeated United 2-0.

April 18th was 'derby' day both in the north east, where Newcastle United faced Sunderland and in Manchester where City entertained United. On Tyneside, Sunderland took both points in a 3-1 win, meanwhile 40,000 at Hyde Road failed to see either net bulge. Newcastle were also to lose their final game of the season, their fifth in the final seven fixtures. It was only fractionally better down Manchester way as Aston Villa won 2-1 at Clayton, Halse and a rare Stacey goal secured a point at Bolton, with the curtain coming down on April 25th with a 3-1 victory over Preston North End at Clayton.

Prior to that final fixture of the season, 'Mancunian' in the *Cricket and Football Field* wrote:

> *"I must confess that on present form the United are a poor lot, and one can hardly imagine them as champions. But that the luck is against them is very apparent, for though they overplayed the City they were denied the goals they were full value for, while in the game against the Villa, they had to play with practically ten men all through, for James Turnbull was injured in the first quarter hour and was almost useless afterwards." The correspondent added: "It cannot be said that the followers of the United are enjoying themselves. The team which, in the early months, touched the extreme almost in brilliance and ability, have now gone, nearly to the other extreme in their ineffectiveness. As one of them remarked to me, "We don't seem able do right now; at one time we could not do wrong. During these last two months we have, been unable to play the same team in two consecutive games. Every position in the team (with the exception of outside left) has undergone changes."*

At least the 2-1 victory over Preston North End was

a fitting end to the season, enabling United to create a new record number of points – fifty-two, finishing nine in front of runners-up Aston Villa. It also enabled the curtain to come down in front of their own support, although the ground was only sparsely filled with around 8,000 spectators, compared with the 45,000 and 50,000 who had squeezed in to watch the games against Bury and Chelsea. Those who were in attendance, however, celebrated in fine style, invading the pitch on the final blast of the referee's whistle, congregating in front of the main stand and cheering the victorious players.

Although Saturday April 25th brought their First Division programme to a close, the United players were not allowed to return home following the Preston North End fixture, and a few celebratory drinks, and throw their boots into the cupboard and forget about them for a few weeks, as they were off to London and Chelsea's Stamford Bridge ground, to face Southern League winners Queens Park Rangers in a specially arranged charity match on Monday April 27th.

Such a fixture had been pencilled in for a number of years, but "the senior organisation always returned a polite but firm negative". United, despite a long and often strenuous season were only too happy to be involved, even if they had to pay their own expenses.

The game, and the attendance, was somewhat spoiled by the weather, but the 12,000 who did make their way to Stamford Bridge witnessed and exciting ninety minutes, but were to see only two goals, one for each side, meaning a replay would be required at the start of the following season to see which club could claim ownership for a year of the Sheriff of London Shield.

Although Mangnall's name was missing from many, if

not all, the numerous articles, mentions, that were to appear in the national press of the day, the major contribution that he had made was obvious to all, between the lines. Like this piece in the *Athletic News* on Monday April 27th

> *"Surely Charlie Roberts had good reason to feel a thrill of pride on Saturday night. Little the Darlington youth thought the day he left Grimsby for Manchester that he was to play against Scotland and later to lead one of the greatest sides seen for years to the proud position of League Champions!*
>
> *"Meredith has done much for Manchester United, but Roberts stands out alone, a giant among his comrades. He it was who rescued his club from the Second Division, and again he has done more than any other man to bring League honours to Manchester for the first time."*

As the fixtures became fewer, Mangnall pencilling in each score on the chart that hung on the wall of his cupboard like office at Clayton, the United manager had more than selecting his first choice eleven, overseeing training and whatever else fell under his remit to dwell upon. A move away from the often dire and dismal surroundings of Clayton had been mooted some time ago, but regular meetings and conversations with J. H. Davies had seen matters develop at a steady pace.

The Mangnall/Davies partnership was an ideal combination. The United secretary knew the sporting side of things inside out. He had been at Bolton when they moved from their rather primitive Pike's Lane ground to Burnden Park, but here, with Manchester United and more so the backing of J. H. Davies, he was able to put his views, his vision, onto paper and plan out a new stadium from scratch. Davies knew little, or perhaps it is best said, had known little, about running a football club when he stepped in to save Manchester United, but he was a shrewd businessman, he had money through his brewery business, with more coming in through salt being found on his land, and he also knew that there was money to be made in the game and money to be made in a move away from Clayton.

There was also, like that in many other 'marriages', disagreements, differences of opinions, but for the time being everything in the garden was rosy. It was no secret that Old Trafford was the chosen site to replace Bank Street as United's new home, Davies arguably being more decisive than his manager in selecting the area, central between the industrial area beside the canal and the cricket ground of the same name. An article in the *Nottingham Football News* painted the picture.

> *"MANCHESTER UNITED LEAVING CLAYTON - Many people will note with interest the news that Manchester United will next season migrate to a new home. The old ground at Clayton has never been a popular one with spectators - indeed, the Manchester United Executive freely state that the patronage accorded to the wonderful team they have got together has by no means been in accordance with the merits of the eleven.*
>
> *"Mr. J. H. Davies, however, has taken the club under his wing. They have only had to ask and they have had, and when a new ground was wanted, Mr. Davies immediately purchased a site of over 30 acres contingent to the famous ground at Old Trafford. This should be a popular site, for the Old Trafford district is identified with sport*

and the atmosphere there is different to that of Clayton. I have heard a well-known star say their men suffered heavily from the effects of the fumes from the chemical works in the district. Then we know that the surface was usually in a shocking state. A blade of grass was a rarity, and the clever Manchester United players themselves felt that they were handicapped by the state of the enclosure. It is bad enough now, but it is nothing to what the old Clayton ground was like in Newton Heath's day. I have played there when you practically sunk up to your ankles in black mud, and when there was not a trace of verdure on the field. Grass won't grow at Clayton, but it will at Old Trafford, and the United have done wisely to arrange to move to more genial surroundings.

"They are lucky to be able to migrate at will. The new ground will be magnificently equipped, and will have accommodation for virtually 1000,000 people, with possibilities of expansion. Another happy idea is the provision of a practise ground adjoining."

With the First Division title having been more or less a forgone conclusion, Mangnall could allow himself more time to oversee the plans for moving away from Clayton, something he would have been unable to do had the title race been of a closely fought nature. But during those closing weeks of the season, and indeed the early weeks of 1908, he had been busy formulating other plans. Plans that would also take Manchester United away from

Clayton, but much further afield than across Manchester to Old Trafford, as it would see them journey across the English Channel to Switzerland, Czechoslovakia, Austria and Hungary.

Particular in his running of the club, Mangnall had put some considerable time and effort into such a momentous tour, while it is also without question that J. H. Davies had bankrolled the practically month long tour for some considerable sum.

Despite the itinerary put in place showing Mangnall, his squad of sixteen players and fellow officials due to leave Manchester Central Station on Friday May 1st at 5.50pm, heading for London St Pancras, where they would arrive some four hours later, they had all been at Hyde Road the previous day for the Final of the Manchester Cup, where a solitary Jimmy Bannister goal was enough to defeat Bury and add another piece of silverware to the collection. It was then home to pack the bags and get a good night's sleep.

The tour was a trip into the unknown and also something of massive adventure for everyone involved, many never having ventured out of England, never mind Britain and although Mangnall's schedule was undoubtedly going to prove tiring, there was also plenty of leisure time, with various excursions thrown into the mix.

From London the party left early on the Saturday morning for Paris via Calais where there was an overnight stay before heading for Zurich, arriving there around 8.00pm on Monday 3rd after an eleven hour journey. This was to be their base until Wednesday 6th according to the official itinerary, but what is missing from the itinerary is a mention of a game in Zurich with details of a 4–2 victory appearing in the national press, although some give the final score as 4-1. Either way it was a United victory with Alec Bell writing home:

> *"The Zurich men went for all they were worth and knocked us about to some tune, but we escaped without injury, and after getting four goals we changed our team. Moger played inside right with Meredith. Turnbull and Bannister went full back, and Wall took goal. It was funny - especially Moger forward. The crowd simply went mad on 'Billy' (Meredith). He was up to all sorts of tricks, and at one time had three of them running after him. At the finish the three of them walked away, and no wonder."*

The first scheduled game had been planned for May 9th against Slavia Prague and 5,000 witnessed a 2-0 victory and such was United's performance that the following day the crowd doubled for the second game between the sides and the visitors did not disappoint with a 4-1 win. Victories against Bohemians [4-0], Fist Vienna [5-0] and a Vienna Select [4-0] followed before the tour erupted into life in Budapest.

May 22nd found United face to face with Ferencvaros, winning 6-2, maintaining their unbeaten run and two days later the sides met again. The score line was little different, 7-0 to the tourists, but the circumstances surrounding the victory were completely different. During the second half, with the score at 6-0, the crowd decided that United were not playing fair and were infringing the rules of the game. Initially the referee thought likewise, but then decided otherwise, although at one point he was considering sending off three United players, only to be surrounded by United players who attempted to explain matters. By now the crowd were quite irritated, more so as the favourites were in for a second big defeat in days and so proceeded to pelt the United players with stones thinking that they were attempting to attack the match official. For some fifteen minutes disorder prevailed and interpreters were required in an attempt to sort matters out and with apologies offered all round, the game restarted and United scored a seventh in partial darkness.

As the teams made their way off the pitch things turned nasty, with an observer being quoted in the *Athletic News* as saying: *"Most of the rioters were repulsive looking Jews, with ungovernable vicious tempers."* Harry Moger was struck across the shoulders with a stick, Stacey was spat upon, with Roberts and Picken also assaulted. Police then charged the rioters and some twenty or so were arrested and dragged into a temporary police station inside the ground. In the United dressing room stones crashed through the windows and when they were ready to leave the ground, mounted police were required to escort them to their hotel, as the assembled crowd numbered some 5,000.

Having managed to get into their carriages it looked as though everything would be fine, but once they began to move, they were caught in a shower of bricks, stones and mud. Bell, Picken, Thomson, Wall and the *Athletic News* correspondent, whoever he was, were hit, as was Ernest Mangnall, and further arrests were made, with the police compelled to draw their swords. Everyone was more than relieved to see their hotel hove into view and even more so that the journey home would soon be undertaken. The United party returned home via Berlin, arriving back in Manchester on May 29th tired, but full of memories to regale their families and friends until it was time to resume pre-season training.

Looking back on the ground breaking tour, Billy Meredith was to write:

>*"Manchester United had some amusing experiences during the tour. In one match we had an excited referee who ruled the game from the touch line. He never came inside the field of play at all, but dashed madly up and down the line. Some of us were laughing so hard we could not play.*
>
>*"The keenness of all our opponents was surprising and the manner in which they hurled themselves at us somewhat disconcerting. In one match an excited referee was going to order two of our men off through a complete misunderstanding, and in another the crowd stoned us as we left the field. But the players we met were, on the whole, a cheery, sporting set, and they did their best to make us at home and to help us to enjoy ourselves.*
>
>*"The one place our boys did not relish was Zurich, where everyone looks fierce, and you expect to see gleaming knives under the long cloaks the men wear. We had a great time at Lucerne and other places, and one night, after the Swiss had sung their Tyrolean songs, we gave them "Eileen Alannah" with might and main. It was one of the funniest scenes imaginable.*
>
>*"In the game at Zurich, I actually had two players who never left me from start to finish. They would have followed me through the town. I had a great time with them. I was much astonished at the size of the crowds and at the money that was taken at the matches at Prague, Vienna, and*

Budapest - they have popular teams in all these places. The least charge for admission was a kroner, which I think represents ninepence or tenpence, and there were seven, eight and ten thousand people at the matches. These clubs can afford to give a good guarantee and if the authorities out there wish to make the game go ahead, they should circulate and create interest in the laws of the game and get a referees' association or society, which will see to it that the games are governed strictly. The grounds I found excellent, and generally in compliance with the regulations save that they were too narrow. Most of the tackle and appliances are bought in England although there is a large manufacturing concern in Zurich.

"Many of the men I played against had good ideas, and, with their wonderful enthusiasm, they would soon improve greatly, were they coached and pulled up at the right time. One obstacle which the game will have to overcome is the lack of ballast found in the multitudes there. Warm-blooded are these people, over-generous in friendship, quickly raised to the height of anger. I saw sufficient to become convinced that the people needed to be schooled in the laws of the game as well as the players and referees. Just as they have faults, these people of Vienna, Budapest, Prague and so on, have qualities and in courtesy and anxiety to give us an excellent time they would need a deal of beating. If you tell the player you are speaking to, or give him to understand, that you like his neck tie, he will at once pull it off and hand it to you with a smile and a bow. How different the Britisher! He *would say: "Yes, it's all right, isn't it?" and point out where you could go and buy one.*

"Speaking of crowd difficulty on the Continent that I have hinted at, I believe it is a fact that the Slavia team at Prague and the Bohemian team of the same old city have not met for years. Do you know why? They dare not. This is a fact. So bitter is the racial feeling that there would assuredly be serious trouble an' these two rivals met. The best part of the teams I saw was, in every case, the defence. Where a good kick would suffice and control of the ball was not much needed. Still, there was not a team of any repute who had not a really good player in their ranks."

One story that Meredith did not relate was that following the game in Budapest he was approach by a supporter and asked for his boots. A bargain was struck and the boots changed hands for the sum of £2.15s.

It wasn't just the players and the men of the press who were to re-tell their adventures, as Mangnall himself went to print. He was to say that the refereeing the matches had not been at all satisfactory and after one game in Vienna, at the express request of the president of the home club, who said he would like to see an Englishman officiate, he undertook control, a second engagement which took take place on the return journey from Budapest, en-route for Berlin. The appointed day arrived, and true to his promise Mangnall went into the centre. All went well up to the interval, and then a little incident occurred which led Mangnall to believe that he had made a distinct hit, and created a profound impression, for one of the officials of the Vienna dub dashed to the field, and after a most theatrical display in gestures presented him with a neat little paper parcel.

Not wishing to delay the re-start, the parcel was thrust into his pocket and the game proceeded and United won 1-0. At full-time, however, he was fiercely assailed by the Vienna club president and charged with permitting all sorts of offences and allowing United to win the game.

Such was the torrent of abuse, Mangnall lost his temper and felt so aggrieved that he suggested that he would bring his team back out onto the field and defeat their opponents by as many goals as the Vienna officials cared to suggest. The offer was turned down.

It was only when driving away from the ground that Mangnall remembered the half time incident and took the small parcel from his pocket and upon opening it found a beautifully inscribed cigarette case. Upon seeing the gift, Billy Meredith was to comment that it was just as well he was given if at half time, as he would not have got it at full time!

His surprise move to well-heeled Manchester United brought different problems, not least the need to improve the playing staff. This is a typical plea posted in the Athletic News.

Mr Mangnall (left under the bowler hat) with the Manchester United team that won promotion in 1905-06.

It's hard to imagine Pep Guardiola endorsing 'Push Ball' as ideal pre-season preparation for his star-studded Manchester City squad but Ernest Mangnall clearly saw the benefits in both fitness to his Manchester United squad and publicity for the club.

Bolton Evening News - Monday Aug 5th 1907

7: UP FOR THE CUP

I T WAS BACK TO REALITY for Ernest Mangnall and his players, although throughout the tour, one unnamed player had pined for home and no sooner had the United secretary/manager returned home, rejoiced in seeing family and friends again and recounted the stories and sights of the European adventure, then it was back to the different surroundings of dear old Clayton.

On his desk, there was the odd contract to sort out, players such as Donnelly and Linkson were added to the playing staff, while the proposed move to Old Trafford also took up much of his time and was very much a matter of not simply of some necessity, but also a concern.

There had been some debate in regards to the proposed move away from Clayton, much to Mangnall's annoyance, but at last, the project was in the hands of Archibald Leitch, the Glaswegian responsible for the construction and re-construction of numerous notable stadiums and it was reported that it was going to cost in the region of £20,000, a considerable sum for a club that not too long ago was practically penniless. There was only one real decision remaining to be made and that was as to whether or not a cemented cycle track would be installed around the playing pitch. This was something that Mangnall was obviously very much in favour of, not simply from his long association with that sport, but such a thing would be hugely beneficial, not simply for local cyclists, but for the hosting of events such as the World Professional Athletic Championship which Mangnall had overseen at Clayton that July, when the Australian A. B. Postle had met an Englishman by the name of W. Growcott, an event witnessed by 10,000 people.

One thing for certain was that Clayton would remain United's home for the whole of the 1908-09 season. It had been hoped that the season might have been brought to a close at the new home, but there was no possibility whatsoever of that happening and it was put back to September 1909 and by the end of 1908. In the meantime the Bank Street ground had been sold to the Manchester Corporation who had an electricity generating station adjacent to the ground and the Town Clerk had negotiated with J. H. Davies over the purchase of the ground, an area of 18,800 square yards, for a sum of £5,500.

With the new season only a matter of days away Mangnall signed a player who at that time would not exactly set the heather on fire, but an individual who, once his playing days came to an end, would remain at the club in an administrative capacity for over fifty years. His name was Harold Hardman who went on to become chairman of the club in the 1950s. Strangely Hardman, who always played as an amateur and who had gained half a dozen England caps, had told the club he couldn't play every week but had also joined the amateurs of Northern Nomads.

Having sought the permission of the Football League to have medals made for the championship winning players, these were presented to the players, trainers and to Harry Stafford following the annual club trial match and the most eagerly looked forward to event on the Manchester United calendar, a summer evening at the home of J. H. Davies.

Mangnall selected his first United line-up of the new

season on Saturday August 29th for the F.A. Charity Shield replay against Queens Park Rangers at Chelsea's Stamford Bridge ground, the first game played at the tail end of the previous season having ended 1-1. This time there was no doubting the winners, with a Jimmy Turnbull hat trick, and a George Wall effort enough to see the name of Manchester United the first to be engraved on the trophy. It was a victory that set the stage for what was to become a memorable season.

Having got the taste for silverware, with the League Championship and Charity Shield now residing at Clayton, Mangnall and his players wanted more and as the 1908-09 season got underway it looked as though it would have to be a top-notch side to snatch the crown from the reigning champions. The campaign kicked off on September 5th with Charity Shield hat-trick hero Jimmy Turnbull scoring ten goals in the first five fixtures. Two on the opening day in the 3-0 win over Preston North End at Deepdale was followed by another double in a 2-1 win over Bury at Clayton, he then hit four in the 6-3 victory over Middlesbrough and one in each of the two fixtures that followed – a 2-1 win over Manchester City and a 3-2 victory over Liverpool. The First Division table had already taken on a familiar look, with United and Newcastle sharing top spot, Turnbull's goals and not numerical order, ensuring United were first. The Geordies had also played a game more.

October, however, was a different kettle of fish altogether. The month opened with a 2-2 draw at Bury, followed by a 2-1 win against Sheffield United at Clayton. Top spot remained United's but then came something of a hiccup. Aston Villa took both points with a 3-1 win in Birmingham, Nottingham Forest left Clayton with a point and Sunderland hit six with only one coming in reply in the north-east, then Chelsea opened November with a 1-0 win at Clayton. For the first time in quite a while when Ernest Mangnall looked at the First Division league table his teams name was not at the top.

Injuries had certainly played their part in the recent blip with a total of twenty-one players having been employed over those opening eleven games, while 'Mancunian' wrote in the *Cricket and Football Field* of Saturday October 17th of Mangnall's team:

> *"The fact of having the reputation of being Champions of the League necessitates constant striving to play up to that reputation, and this is no easy task, for, in addition to being constantly at high pressure, all our opponents seem to be imbued with the spirit of Jack-the-Giant-Killer, and would glory in our downfall. When they meet they put forth their best efforts. Of course, the longer we hold our present position under such circumstances the greater the credit, but I do not wonder that occasionally our team lags a bit, and that the strain tells on them."*
>
> *"It is no use disguising the fact that the United are not playing as well as they did this time last year, and beyond the fact that they are not losing, there is not a great deal to enthuse over. Of course, our team has not yet been able to settle down owing to injuries, &c."*

A matter of weeks later, following defeats at the hands of Sunderland and Chelsea, that same correspondent penned:

> *"The truth of the old saying that 'it never rains but*

it pours' is being plainly exemplified in the affairs of the United just now, as troubles are falling thick and fast upon us. In fact, we struck an avalanche (or vice versa) last week-end. The shock then received was the most severe for years, and will take some little time to recover from." This was echoed in the Lancashire Evening Post – "United are just now in a rather bad way through injuries and the absence of reserves of anything like the class of the men who are laid aside. Such men as Roberts, Burgess and "Sandy" Turnbull are not readily replaced."

No mention could be found anywhere in relation to the man at the helm not doing his job, such was his reputation, not just at Clayton, but within the game in general but just as quickly as the results went in reverse, there was once again forward movement, with only two defeats from the eight fixtures that took United up to the end of 1908. One of those defeats came against title hopefuls Newcastle United, losing 2-1 on Tyneside on Christmas Day, but twenty-four hours later, revenge was sweet with a solitary Harold Halse goal enough to claim victory at Clayton in the reverse fixture. The other defeat had come at the hands of another club with their eyes on the First Division title, Everton, who claimed victory by the odd goal in five at Goodison.

That Boxing Day victory against Newcastle at Clayton brought down the curtain on a momentous year for Manchester United and who was to say that despite having lost five games in the first half of the season, the championship could not be retained. The league table showed United in third place with twenty-six points from nineteen fixtures. Newcastle were second, twenty-seven points from twenty fixtures, while Everton claimed top spot with thirty points from twenty fixtures. Neither was anyone to say that the flow of silverware could not continue, with the elusive F. A. Cup about to make its annual appearance on the fixture list.

January 1909 began in grand style with a 4–3 victory over Notts County at Clayton. Sandy Turnbull had returned to the fray while Halse was finding the net with some regularity, but despite this ideal start, defeats were just around the corner. Preston took both points from the January 2nd fixture at Clayton with a 2–0 win, while the journey back from Middlesbrough a week later was a long one, having suffered a 5–0 defeat. Not the best of preparations for the forthcoming F. A. Cup first round tie against Brighton and Hove Albion at Clayton.

Manchester United's F. A. Cup life had stretched from the match official awarding the tie to their opponents in their first venture in the competition against Fleetwood Rangers in 1886–87 because the Newton Heath players refused to play extra time, to 7–0 successes against the likes of West Manchester and Accrington in 1896–97 and 1902–03, although the furthest they had ever ventured in the competition had been in 1905–06 and 1907–08 when they faltered when only a step away from a place in the semi-finals.

Preceding Brighton and Hove Albion out of the hat at least gave United home advantage, but the Clayton pitch was to be found in its usual mid-season condition, which was basically a field heavy of mud, allowing for little in the way of quality of football being produced. On the morning of Brighton's visit, snow and sleet had fallen prior to kick-off adding to the misery of the surroundings. The weather certainly played its part in there being a relatively poor attendance, while the lack of bodies passing through the gates was not helped by the fact that Manchester City were also at home against Tottenham Hotspur, with the *Manchester Evening News* correspondent writing; *"That the Manchester public will not go to Clayton if they can get their football elsewhere was illustrated today when the English Cup tie with Brighton was played"*. A truth which highlighted the directorate's wisdom in planning a move away from the chemical coated mud bath for the fresh air of Trafford Park, then the world's first industrial estate!

The cup-tie at Clayton was not a game for the faint hearted, with the north–south divide adding some additional spice to the fixture and at times it looked as though some of the players would actually come to blows. Play often overstepped the laws of the game and at different times during the ninety minutes Jimmy Turnbull, Alec Bell and Vince Hayes of United and Martin of Brighton were off the field having various injuries tended to by their respective trainers.

As it turned out Brighton, although putting up a spirited performance, were no match on the day for United who attacked with much regularity, making the game, particularly in the closing stages, into something of a rather one sided affair. However the visitor's rigid defence coupled with the poor state of the ground made accurate football almost impossible, and forced numerous errors from both sides, keeping scoring to a minimum. Although to be fair to the twenty-two players, despite the ankle deep mud and play having to be stopped on a regular basis so that the players could have the mud wiped from their faces after heading the ball which became heavier as the game progressed, the overall play at times was considered by the *Manchester Evening News* reporter to be of "a fairly high standard".

A meagre crowd of 8,074, who paid some £235 8s 3d, were rewarded for their endurance in watching what was described as the poorest game at Clayton this season with only one goal, scored on the half hour mark, the result of three passes which took the ball from United's half and into the back of the Brighton net. Jimmy Turnbull pushed the ball wide to Meredith, who quickly crossed it into the Brighton goalmouth. Atkinson had the opportunity to clear his lines, but whether due to the conditions or otherwise, miss-kicked and Halse pounced, beating goalkeeper Whiting with a hard low drive between the two Brighton full backs and into the corner of the net.

On reflection United did well to go in at the interval a goal in front, mainly due to having played for the majority of the first half with only ten men, Hayes and Jimmy Turnbull both off the field at different times for lengthy periods. The latter had also been involved in an exchange of words with Stewart, an encounter which rumbled on all afternoon and which eventually led to the footballing side of the game disintegrating.

Minor knocks had to be attended to before Bell left the field with a head injury, again leaving United with ten men, but soon after his re-appearance the home side were forced to play with a man short on a more permanent basis. Stewart, the Brighton left back and captain had tussled with Billy Meredith throughout the opening forty-five minutes and after the United winger had ghosted past Atkinson and sped down the wing, Stewart stepped in and robbed the Welshman of the ball. The Brighton defender then dribbled the ball down the touchline, but in the direction of his own goal, before for some unknown reason kicking it out of play. Out of frustration more than anything else, Meredith proceeded to kick the Brighton player with the side of his foot.

There was certainly no malice in the rather unnecessary attack, but it left the referee with little choice than to send the Welshman off. Referee Lewis of Rotherham was immediately surrounded by United players, including Meredith who claimed that he had been provoked, but despite a prolonged and heated exchange the official refused to back down and the outside right made his way to the dressing rooms. It was considered by many to be a harsh decision, with the incident that led to the dismissal not as severe as much of what had gone before.

Stewart himself was soon to follow Meredith off the pitch, carried off with a leg injury, following an encounter with Jimmy Turnbull. Was this an accident or revenge?

The referee himself came in for much criticism due to his handling of the game and was booed off at the end, despite the home team's victory. The *Manchester Evening News* correspondent wrote: *"The game was spoiled by the referee, who allowed the players to get out of hand. A number of unpleasant incidents that went un-noticed and in no previous match this season have the United had so many men hurt. Twice Meredith was thrown head long into the hoarding, whilst one kick split open his shin guard and caused a wound several inches in length"*.

To their credit Brighton came close on a few occasions and did have opportunities to equalise. A header from Martin hitting the top of the United cross bar. But their half backs failed to offer their fellow forwards much in the way of support. Had they done so, then a replay would certainly not have been out of the question but it was United, inspired by Charlie Roberts, for whom the conditions caused fewer problems, who went into the draw for Round Two.

Seven days after that cup success against Brighton, neighbours City were beaten 3-1 at Clayton with Mangnall's new signing, George Livingstone from Glasgow Rangers, notching a double. The player was familiar to Mangnall having been an F.A. Cup winner with Manchester City in 1903-04 and had two Scottish caps to his name, and now he didn't only have the distinction of playing for both Manchester clubs, but also for both Auld Firm clubs. Livingstone, along with his United team mates, was back in Glasgow a matter of hours after the victory over City arriving on Clydeside to the sound of four pipers who escorted the team and officials, along with a large throng of onlookers, to the city's Alexandra Hotel, prior to a friendly against a Glasgow Select XI on Monday 25th.

The game in question was a charity fixture, arranged by comedian George Robey and included a race from the Theatre Royal to Ibrox, something that would undoubtedly have been of much interest to Mangnall. The ninety minutes football was certainly of interest to Glasgow football supporters and despite it being an afternoon kick-off it still managed to attract 12,000 supporters, paying over £333 for the privilege of being there.

Such was United manager Ernest Mangnall's disgust with the referee who had officiated at the Brighton cup-tie that he wrote a letter of complaint to the Football Association prior to Meredith's disciplinary hearing, saying:

> *"We have never yet reported a referee, for we recognise that their duties are onerous and often unpleasant, but I must say that Mr Lewis proved very weak and did not appear to have the slightest*

control of the players. The Brighton and Hove officials agreed, and their players pleaded hard to the referee for Meredith to be allowed to remain on the field. I may point out that Mr Lewis's weakness was the same in the Notts County match on New Year's Day and we have asked the Football League not to appoint him to any of our matches.

"We should be prepared to produce evidence to prove his inefficiency and in our opinion his conduct was such as to encourage players in the act of wrong doing. As practical followers of the game, members of the Association know what it means when players are allowed to get out of hand. We trust that under the circumstances, and especially recognising that it was Meredith's first offence in such a long career, you will deal leniently with him."

Strong words indeed but Mangnall, however, was far from confident that his letter would be enough to persuade those members to be lenient, as along with his pleading letter, he also sent a deposit in view of an appeal against what the secretary hoped would be a modest fine against his star man. As it turned out Mangnall saw his deposit returned, along with a communication that there was no possibility of an appeal and that Meredith had been suspended for a month. This may have been seen as the FA getting their own back on one of their fiercest critics as the incident itself was hardly worthy of dismissal in the first place. Nevertheless it represented a huge blow to United's hopes as Meredith would miss league games against Sheffield United and Nottingham Forest and the F. A. Cup tie against Everton as well as a potential third round tie. He would also miss a Welsh international trial.

The first of the Meredith-less fixtures was the second round F. A. cup-tie against Everton at Clayton, a game of an entirely different aspect to Brighton's visit in the previous round. Where Brighton were a Southern League side, Everton were serious championship challengers who sat just three points behind leaders Newcastle at the top of the First Division. As for United's title hopes, they had taken a severe knock the week prior to the cup-tie against Everton losing 3-1 defeat at Anfield to Liverpool.

In the week leading up to the cup-tie Mangnall could only hope that the players who were carrying knocks would be fit to play whilst deliberating over who would replace his Welsh talisman, as somewhat surprisingly, he had no immediate replacement within the ranks. In the end Halse moved from leading the front line to the outside-right spot, Livingstone recovered from his injury and took the inside-right position, with the two Turnbull's and Wall making up the attacking front five.

Compared with the feeble 8,000 odd who had made their way to Clayton for the Brighton tie, there were over 35,000 present for this Lancashire battle, with stand tickets selling out well before the day of the match. The gates opened at 1.00 for the 3.30 kick-off, with large queues already outside and the Manchester Tramway Company enjoyed a highly profitable afternoon ferrying supporters towards the Clayton ground, although many who could not afford both the fare and the cost of admission, preferred to walk from the city centre.

As per usual there was not a blade of grass to be seen on the pitch, but the Clayton ground staff, to their credit, managed to get the surface in excellent condition due to more than a sprinkling of sand, which at least gave the players something of a foothold.

Both goals saw considerable activity, as the first half bubbled into action. Wall broke clear from the half way line, but with only Scott in the Everton goal to beat, a huge groan was to emerge from the majority of the packed enclosure as the 'keeper dived and pushed the ball against the post before it was scrambled to safety. A couple of overhead kicks from the United outside left were also cleared, while at the opposite end Moger was kept on his toes and it was a surprise to many that the home goal remained intact. An Everton free-kick was cleared by the United defence, with Sandy Turnbull swinging the ball out to Wall just over the halfway line. The winger proceeded to dribble his way down the wing and from just inside the penalty area, hit a tremendous shot which Scott in the Everton goal managed to palm onto the upright before McConnachie scrambled the ball clear. At the opposite end a centre from Sharp saw Moger pull off a fine save, but he could only palm the ball out and amid a goalmouth scramble before the ball was eventually cleared.

With play evenly matched it looked as though the stalemate would continue into the second half, but with half time approaching the two Turnbulls moved down-field, with Sandy picking out Wall on the left. The winger sent a high centre into the Everton goalmouth and McConnachie attempted to clear but the ball was blocked by Livingstone and from a position down by the goal line he flicked the ball over his head and into the path of Halse, who met it firmly on his left foot, blasting it over the heads of the defenders and past a helpless Scott to give United the lead.

United resumed the second half where they left off and any Everton attacks were confidently dealt with, but the presence of Meredith was sorely missed as United lacked any real penetration, especially down the right. The visitors on the other hand played well in defence but were poor upfront with their forwards preferring to see the whites of Moger's eyes before shooting, although in the dying minutes they almost snatched a draw, but after getting the better of Hayes, Sharp shot into the side netting. Somewhat miraculously, in the opinion of many, United held on to their lead and that solitary goal was enough to see them into the Third Round.

Despite the lack of goals it had been a commendable victory and one that would give the team confidence for the road ahead, but that confidence was to take a knock, a severe one at that, as the two February First Division fixtures, both away from home, produced only one point, from the 0-0 draw at Sheffield United, while the trip to Nottingham Forest ended in a 2-0 reverse.

Hopes of retaining the title now looked bleak despite there still being a dozen fixtures to play and when Mangnall looked at the First Division table, he would find his team in fourth place, ten points behind leaders Newcastle United and six behind second place Everton. Nothing was impossible, but it was quite a gap to make up, with the two front runners having to drop a considerable number of points.

Failing to score in successive league fixtures for the second time in a matter of weeks was somewhat unusual for United, but what made this recent pair of blank Saturday afternoon's even stranger was the fact that sandwiched in between those blanks at Sheffield and Nottingham was a resounding 6-1 F. A. Cup third round victory over Blackburn Rovers. The 35,000 plus crowd that had flocked to Clayton for the Everton tie was bettered by some three thousand for the Lancashire head-to-head. It was also expected to be a testing encounter as Blackburn Rovers had something of an F. A. Cup a pedigree, having won it a joint record five times.

An hour and a half prior to the 3.30pm kick-off there were already over 15,000 in the ground, with a sizable contingent having travelled from the Blackburn area. The limited reserved stand seats, priced at five shillings, had sold out quickly and a few minutes after 3.00pm it was advised that the gates be shut, even though there were still hundreds outside. Such was the mass of bodies within the tight and compact ground, many found a vantage point on top of the stand roof, which not only allowed them an excellent view of the proceedings it kept them well away from the crush of bodies below, with countless unfortunate supporters fainting due to the pressure in front of the stand and on the banking along the other sides of the ground.

United were on the attack from the offset with a strong sun behind them and Bell sent the ball down the left flank towards Sandy Turnbull who in turn picked out George Wall, but the imminent danger was cleared by Cowell. Roberts then sent over a free kick, but a header from Halse was also cleared by the Rovers defence. Continuing to attack a centre from Halse was headed into the goalmouth by Sandy Turnbull, but just as Jimmy Turnbull was about to reach it, Ashcroft managed get his foot to the ball and nudge it away. At the opposite end Blackburn's first attack saw Anthony make progress down the left, but Latheron fired over. Aitkenhead missed from close range, and then another opportunity was shunned after Cameron gained possession from a throw in, but although his centre dropped invitingly in front of the

United goal for Davies, Moger dashed from his line to clear the danger. But with ten minutes gone, the deadlock was broken. Wall and Sandy Turnbull manoeuvred the ball forward and on to the United right and from there Halse found the advancing Wall, who calmly trapped the ball, passing to Sandy Turnbull little more than three yards from goal to score easily. A head injury to the goal scorer forced him from the pitch minutes later, but even reduced to ten men United held firm, although the visitors slowly pushed them onto the defensive, missing three good opportunities to snatch an equaliser. Full backs Hayes and Stacey were often stretched, whilst Moger made countless outstanding saves to keep United in front.

The second half got underway in spectacular fashion, with Wall flashing a shot narrowly wide of the post a mere two minutes after the re-start, but the crowd had only a further minute to wait for that second goal to materialise. As Blackburn attacked the United defenders appealed for off-side against Crompton and for some unknown reason the England man stopped, perhaps expecting the referee to award a free kick against him, but the ball was soon passed to Jimmy Turnbull who bore down on the Blackburn goal. Sensing the danger Ashcroft moved quickly off his line in order to block the United man's advance, but it was to little avail, as the ball was slipped past him and into the net. It was now all United and Livingstone soon made it 3-0, his shot from twenty yards out beating Ashcroft, who could only get a hand to it as it dipped under the crossbar. Thoroughly disheartened Blackburn somehow managed to pull a goal back through Davies, although they were seldom in the picture and it was only a matter of time before they found themselves further behind, Sandy Turnbull adding a fourth with a low drive, followed five minutes later by a fifth from the other Turnbull in the United front line who ran through the Rovers defence single handed to score. With one minute remaining United rubbed in their superiority with a sixth, Sandy Turnbull claiming his hat-trick.

Despite the score line, there had not been much between the sides, the main difference being the different styles of play rather than the individual skills of the players on view. One well-rehearsed ploy adopted by United saw them make a short pass in front of the Blackburn goal, which would see one red shirted player make the pretence of going to shoot, but proceeding to step over the ball, deceiving the defenders and allowing it to roll to a team mate, thus creating, if it came off, an opening.

How United managed to go from scoring six to failing to find the net in the next game is anyone's guess, but a bigger question was soon to be asked as to why the league champions could go from swatting aside everyone who came their way to struggling through ninety minutes of football. Not only that, but also struggling to score goals. There was no suggestion that the half dozen scored against Blackburn Rovers was a fluke, but in the league, March and the beginning of April proved to be a disaster for manager and team alike.

The Saturday after Blackburn were hit for six, Forest scored two without reply, then came a 1-1 draw against Chelsea, then another share of the points – 2-2 at home to Sunderland. It was after this that the walls crumbled, confidence took a beating and the goals for column remained the same for 360 minutes, despite having Billy Meredith back in the side as successive home defeats to Blackburn Rovers, who gained revenge for their cup defeat with a 3-0 win, Aston Villa (2-0) and Bristol

City [1-0] prefaced a 2-0 defeat to Sheffield Wednesday. Those results left United foundering in ninth place. The reigning champions were now sixteen points drift of leaders Newcastle United.

In the F. A. Cup, however, a completely different picture was painted. Round four conjured up yet another Lancashire 'derby' with Mangnall returning to the familiar surroundings of Turf Moor, Burnley on March 6th, knowing full well that his old club would certainly not be in a generous mood, despite everything he had done for them, whilst at the same time, he had also to lift his troops following defeat at Forest.

It is said that an element of good luck is required to win the FA Cup, which is probably true as the draw for each round is simply a lottery, but it was luck of a different kind that was bestowed upon Manchester United that Saturday afternoon at Turf Moor. The United players had witnessed Burnley's victory over Tottenham Hotspur in the previous round, so they knew what to expect, while the Burnley officials also knew what to expect - a bumper crowd, so in an effort to squeeze more spectators into the ground and earn some extra cash, they dismantled one of the stands, moving it back several yards, allowing for an additional 6,000 or so to be accommodated, pushing the ground capacity to well over 30,000.

The weekend re-construction work was to little avail as heavy over-night frost was followed by snow showers, which by kick-off time had turned to sleet, forcing transport in local areas to more or less grind to a halt, whilst also forcing many to reconsider their plan for the day, with most deciding to remain at home rather than stand in the freezing conditions at Turf Moor. The expected bumper crowd failed to materialise with only 15,471 passing through the gates, hoping for some excitement to warm them up and with the temperature dropping by the minute, they certainly wanted something to make their journey worthwhile.

The pitch was covered in a heavy carpet of snow and it was debatable whether referee H. F. Bamlett would actually start the game, but start it he did and within ten minutes, with the wind and snow behind them, Burnley took the lead. Smethams crossing the ball towards the United goal and Ogden steering the ball into the far corner of the net, well out of the reach of United 'keeper Moger. Undeterred by that early setback and the inclement weather, United managed to make some headway with Sandy Turnbull and Halse forcing Burnley 'keeper Dawson into three excellent saves. The former also had an excellent opportunity to level the score, but took the ball too wide and the final angle was simply too fine to force the ball home. At the other end Ogden hit the post with Moger beaten.

As the second half got underway snow began to fall even heavier, the players finding the conditions far from suitable, but still they plodded on. United, now with the storm behind them, enjoyed the greater percentage of the play, but despite this, they still could not find a way past an extremely resolute Burnley defence. Although enjoying a fair percentage of the play, there were now signs of tiredness allowing the home side to creep back into the game and, with home supporters sensing victory as the game moved towards the final eighteen minutes, they urged the Clarets on.

Their hopes, however, were dealt a crushing blow. A shrill blast from the referee's whistle echoed around the ground, but with no infringement having taken place, players and spectators alike were uncertain as to the official's action. It soon became clear, however, that the referee had simply brought the proceedings to a premature halt.

It was a decision of his own making, as none of the players, despite the awful conditions and with the snow still falling from a leaden sky, had even hinted that the game should be abandoned. Although it was later suggested that the United players had been muttering about having the game brought to a premature end for much of the second half. The weather was still deteriorating, but having endured some seventy-two minutes and having indeed started the game in the first place, it was felt that the referee should have allowed the game to reach its conclusion. Others felt that the referee had done the correct thing.

The people of Burnley held a glimmer of hope that the Football Association would go along with a precedent from an earlier abandoned game, when only the minutes remaining were played out, but there was no possibility of this happening and the game, much to local displeasure, was ordered to be replayed in its entirety.

It is a decision that still rankles the Burnley support over a century later. The fact that afternoon's referee, Herbert Bamlett, later became manager of Manchester United [1927-1931] did nothing to assuage conspiracy theorists, nor his close association with the Players Union. However his decision to abandon the cup-tie didn't do his referring career any harm as he went on to referee the 1914 FA Cup final between Liverpool and Burnley, [and no, the Merseyside club didn't win, Burnley did 1-0] as well as the Scotland v England international that same year.

So the following Wednesday it was back to Turf Moor with just over a thousand more in attendance than had witnessed the first encounter. The pitch for the replay was little better than a quagmire due to a rapid thaw and in all honesty it was in a worse condition than it had been four days previously but despite those adverse conditions United adapted to them much better and Burnley's second bite at the cherry was little more than a nibble, as the visitors, with the wind behind them in the opening forty-five minutes, began strongly. Sandy Turnbull tried to get Wall away on the left, but his pass was too strong and then Roberts also picked out his outside left in the Burnley penalty area, but the United outside left was pulled up for offside, an offence that both sides were fell foul of on numerous occasions. Slowly, the home side began to test the United defence and Moger did well to save from Smethams at the second attempt, the United 'keeper then managing to block another attempt from the same player minutes later. A Wall centre was headed just wide by Jimmy Turnbull and then Duckworth robbed Smethams and sent Halse scurrying forward. His pass, however, got stuck in the mud and Howarth cleared. Moffat gave away a corner with Meredith's kick finding Roberts who managed get a shot on goal, but Dawson managed to stop it on the line.

In the sixteenth minute Burnley took the lead; Smethams, a continuous threat to the United defence, broke away from Stacey while in an obvious offside position and crossed from the right. Moger managed to push the ball onto the post, but much to his dismay, it rebounded to the feet of Ogden who accepted the golden opportunity and tapped the ball into the empty net. Undeterred, United continued to push forward and Burnley left-back McLean had to clear from his own goalmouth on three separate occasions, but it was the home side who were the more dangerous and they almost increased their lead, but Stacey managed to clear the immediate danger.

In the twentieth minute, a Jimmy Turnbull shot had Dawson well beaten, but the ball smashed against the cross bar and Howarth cleared for a corner. The flag kick was only partially cleared by the Burnley defenders, falling to the feet of Halse, who beat McLean before shooting into the far corner of Dawson's net for the equaliser. Within eight minutes United had the advantage; Meredith crossed from the right and Jimmy Turnbull threw himself towards the ball but failed to make contact, the ball broke to Wall who delivered a telling pass into the goalmouth and Jimmy Turnbull made no mistake this time around, finishing the move to put the visitors 2-1 in front. The goal scorer, however, was soon to come in for rough treatment from the Burnley defenders and was injured twice by some over zealous play.

A Meredith shot was almost turned into his own goal by Leake but the resulting corner was cleared to safety, as the visitors piled on the pressure and despite the rather adverse conditions underfoot, the ball was moved about quickly, with the play flowing freely from end to end. Moger saved from Abbott and as play once again swung to the opposite end of the ground, Sandy Turnbull missed an excellent opportunity following some fine play by Halse and Wall.

After the interval, during which the Burnley players had been refreshed with a glass of champagne, there was a strong wind now sweeping around the ground, but the half time liquid refreshment did little to invigorate the home side and indeed had something of the opposite effect, with the home side's game deteriorating badly. Stacey cleared from the ever dangerous Abbott, while McLean just manager to get to the ball before Halse. Leake then headed a Burnley corner just over the United bar. Then Wall broke clean through the Turf Moor defence, but held onto the ball too long, allowing Dawson to race from his goal and save. The Burnley 'keeper then made another excellent save from Jimmy Turnbull, but with seventeen minutes of the second half played he was beaten for the third time by Jimmy Turnbull.

Burnley had adopted the rather strange tactics of attempting to dribble with the ball, coupled with short passes, which due to the conditions was certainly not advised. They were, however, rewarded with a consolation second goal in the dying minutes, when Ogden nudged the ball past Moger amid a goalmouth scramble. By that time the outcome of the game had been a forgone conclusion, mainly due to United's superiority and the Burnley players' inability to reproduce the form of the previous encounter. They were also fortunate not to find themselves even further behind when the referee refused to award United a penalty following a foul on Wall.

The 3-2 victory propelled United into their first ever F A Cup semi-final, but following those goalless league defeats and having been paired in the semi-final with table-toppers Newcastle United, few gave United any chance of reaching the final. The other semi-final between Bristol City and Derby County looked much more favourable. Had their 'cup luck' finally ran out?

Saturday March 27th brought great excitement in Manchester. From early morning until around two o'clock there was a large exodus of supporters from Manchester heading for Bramall Lane, Sheffield and although exact numbers could not be confirmed at the time, it was suspected that *"every follower of the Clayton club who could afford to, availed himself of the opportunity of cheering on the champions to victory."*

Both the Midland and Great Central Railway Companies were stretched to their limit and the officials at Manchester's London Road, Central and Victoria Stations admitted that even during the peak holiday seasons they had never catered for so many people at one time, with one official stating – *"The record exodus of football enthusiasts which was achieved when Manchester City played Sheffield Wednesday in the semi-final round at Everton in the year they won the English Cup* [1904] *was easily eclipsed."* Thankfully the United players, who had been training at Cuddington in leafy Cheshire had kept their departure time a secret and avoided the throngs at the station.

There had been much complaining in and around Sheffield prior to the match due to the admission price being one shilling instead of a more affordable six old pennies, but this certainly did not deter many of the travelling support of both semi-finalists, with a crowd of 40,116 paying a total of £3,590 in gate receipts.

Having won the toss Newcastle, who were favourites to win and who actually claimed that they were, man for man, superior to any other side in the country, played with the sun and a brisk breeze on their backs, but the sun soon disappeared and along with it, the rather slow start to the semi-final, as the players of both sides soon found their momentum and goals came under threat.

In his report of the game for *The Umpire*, C. E. Sutcliffe wrote: *"Both teams received a rare welcome from the crowd, which did not need reminding that the contestants were respectively League champions and prospective League Champions. No amount of personal feeling or rival jealousy can deprive Manchester United of their claim to greatness. Since the advent of their new management, they have won honours and distinction."*

In the opening five minutes Newcastle came close on a couple of occasions to opening the scoring, whilst keeping United on the defensive, their left wing in particular, causing United numerous problems. From a Wilson centre, Higgins drove the ball a few inches wide of Moger's post and then Stewart evaded the United defence, but wasted the opportunity. Offside by both teams also failed to help the flow of the game. United, however, slowly began to find their feet and rhythm and by the twentieth minute had shown enough to make Newcastle aware that the result was far from a foregone conclusion: Wall shot over after getting the better of McCracken, before Moger fumbled a shot from Duncan, which was fortunately cleared as Shepperd moved in. A couple of long drives from Meredith and Wall tested Lawrence in the Newcastle goal, the 'keeper dealing comfortably with both. Several "scrimmages" around that Newcastle goal kept the huge crowd on their toes, but neither side were playing anything like the football that their supporters and the neutrals were usually accustomed to. In United's case, in days of old and not that of recent weeks!

Just before the interval Newcastle lost the services of centre-forward Shepperd with an injury – a blow to the face if you read one report or a sprained ankle if you read another. No matter what the injury actually was, when he returned following the break, he was moved to the left wing where he was totally ineffective. United, however, could not make the advantage of the extra man tell in those closing stages of the first half.

Although Newcastle returned to full strength after the interval, it was their opponents who made the early running and despite the advantage held by Mangnall's men, they seldom caused Lawrence in the Newcastle goal much in the way of trouble. It soon became obvious to the Newcastle support that despite being back to full strength, Sheppard was limping badly and could be considered little more than a passenger, but the favourites continued to cause the United rear-guard problems and a pass to Wilson saw Hayes having to be alert to clear the danger. Roberts headed against the Newcastle bar, but then Sandy Turnbull limped off for treatment and when he returned, moved to the wing. Stewart was only inches wide with a fine effort. With twenty-five minutes of the second half gone United's superiority finally told. After Wall and Jimmy Turnbull missed chances to break the deadlock, the former moved down the left before centring the ball and as two players tussled for the ball Halse nipped in and drove the ball hard past a helpless Lawrence.

As the afternoon wore on the pitch became rather slippy and as the light began to fade playing conditions were far from ideal. Halse should have scored a second from a Wall centre, but his effort was blocked by the Newcastle custodian. United clung their slim advantage as the minutes ticked away, with Newcastle pushing forward in search of a last gasp equaliser but with left back Whitson now also injured, they were basically down to nine men and were never going to get the better of a firm United defence. United had made it to the show-piece final at last!

Newcastle had been poor, with their half backs failing

to match the strength of their rivals and whilst he was fit, Shepperd had been easily contained by Charlie Roberts, by far the man of the match, who was according to *The Manchester Guardian* "cool in defence and accurate in his passing and tackling". Even so United were below par, Halse will be remembered only for his goal, Sandy Turnbull was only average, Meredith was well watched, with Jimmy Turnbull always on the move.

Cup finalists for the first time in their history, Mangnall may have conceded the league title without much of a fight but everything could now be focused on a Crystal Palace date against Bristol City. However, even though the final was still some eighteen days away, there were rumours already circulating that the footballing show-piece might not go ahead as planned due to the continuing friction between the Players Union and the Football Association. With United in the final and their players still heavily involved in the Union, this may well have been the foundation on which the rumour was set, but it was soon squashed and all attention quickly swung to the game itself.

Between the Newcastle semi-final and the final United still had seven league fixtures to fulfil and their form continued as it had done in recent weeks, throwing up a mixture of results. Three blank score lines immediately followed that cup success – a 2-0 defeat at home to Aston Villa, a similar defeat at Sheffield Wednesday and a 1-0 reversal at home to cup final opponents Bristol City. A point was finally claimed from a 2-2 draw with Everton at Clayton and another point came from a 0-0 draw in the return match against Bristol followed by the first win in twelve league games – 1-0 against Notts County.

Mangnall, who had been inundated with requests for

Cup Final tickets, had once again to be grateful for having a chairman as understanding and with deep pockets as he had in J. H. Davies. With United playing Leicester City away in the third last league fixture of the season on April 17th, a week prior to the final, United headed south to Chingford, where they would remain until after the Crystal Palace date.

A London correspondent for the *Manchester Evening News* caught up with Mangnall and his players at their headquarters only to find them aimlessly hitting golf balls here, there and everywhere and when he put the question to the United manager that Chingford was not the ideal place to prepare for a Cup Final, he was hit with the reply:

> *"Not a good place! Of course, it is. It is good enough for anything. Here we have the open country and splendid air. Where will you find better? I know some people think we ought to have remained at Cuddington. But they are not the people who have had anything to do with football training and management. This is where Everton trained when they won the Cup. It is where Tottenham Hotspur trained when they succeeded and surely what is good enough for them to win ought to serve Manchester United as well."*

"They tell me the climate is relaxing," continued Mr. Mangnall, *"but I have not found it to be so yet, and with the food our lads put out of sight, I should think we could do with something relaxing. They won't take any harm here with golf every day and occasional spins when we find it necessary to keep up their speed."*

Looking forward to the final, United's secretary added: *"I am sorry to see that the Bristol centre forward* [Sam Gilligan] *got hurt the other day. I hope that it will still be possible for him to recover sufficiently to be able to take his part in the great match. Nothing would please us more than to meet the best team Bristol City can bring to meet us, and I am sure they would like to meet our best. So far as I can see there is nothing to prevent us putting the best men we have in the field, only, of course, you cannot tell what will happen so far ahead."*

As could be expected, interest in the final was high and on the Friday evening prior to the big day, the Manchester Railway stations were a hive of activity, excursions to the capital having been advertised at eleven shillings for a day return. If the exodus to Sheffield for the semi-final tie had surpassed anything previously, then that particular Friday evening saw scenes the likes of which had never been previously witnessed. *"This has been one of the warmest times I have ever experienced,"* proclaimed one over-worked station master, *"I never remember such large crowds outward bound for one place, and all my staff, I can assure you, have had to exercise all their ingenuity to deal with them"*

As the Town Hall clock struck ten, an hour before the first train was due to depart from Manchester, the first large group of United supporters made their way to London Road Station. Slowly the platforms began to fill, but when another contingent of around 800 supporters appeared, the area was at bursting point.

Reports of the time tell of the supporters having "every conceivable kind of musical instrument that could possibly be carried", with the noise making it extremely difficult for the station staff to tell the crowds what platform they should be making their way to. It was estimated that around 30,000 left Manchester on that Friday night and in the early hours of the Saturday morning.

For one party of boisterous supporters panic set in.

No, they had not left their precious tickets at home, they had left their 'refreshments' on the 'wagonette' that had brought them to the station. Thankfully, due to the crowds outside, it had not moved and it was with much relief that the bottled beer, numerous cases of whisky and of lesser importance, some sandwiches and pies were secured for the journey ahead.

Few, however, were concerned about events in London on the eve of the game that had nothing at all to do with the final. United, along with Fulham and Newcastle United, were up before the League Management Committee charged with playing a weakened team. Fulham were fined £50, Newcastle £25, while United were, for the time being, not investigated due to Mangnall not being able to appear owing to the events of the following afternoon. Their case would be heard on another day.

United travelled to Liverpool Street Station on the morning of the match from their Chingford headquarters where they had lunch at the nearby Great Eastern Hotel, before making the journey to Crystal Palace, which due to the vast crowds took the best part of an hour. Leading up to the kick off the traffic from central London out to Sydenham was like a giant snake, crawling its way towards the ground. Taxis and buses stretched back for over a mile, with the ground itself quickly filling up, many securing a rather precarious vantage point on trees surrounding the vast arena.

As kick-off drew near a number of Bristol City supporters marched along the touch line with a banner proclaiming "Stop the Game, it's snowing. Success to Burnley" to some light-hearted replies from the Mancunian contingent. Others had hoisted a Bristol City flag up a pole, but their opposite numbers attempted to remove it and replace it with another which proclaimed "Play Up Manchester". A United supporter was given a much warmer reception when he emerged from the crowd dressed as a footballer, in United's usual red shirt.

Among the crowd were numerous soldiers in uniform, from members of the Royal Horse Artillery to the Inniskilling Dragoons. Enterprising locals did an excellent trade in charging two shillings for the hire of a soda water box or a barrel, which would offer a better advantage point from which to view the action and for those who did not own such items, they hastily constructed something for the supporter to stand on, with the sound of constant hammering being heard above the shouts of support for both teams. Some constructed 'swinging cradles', like those used in the painting of the side of a ship, fastening them onto the front of the stand and charging the sum of one shilling per 'cradle'. On the whole supporters were in good humour, but there were some twenty-two arrests. Sixteen of those were for gambling offences, with tricksters luring unsuspecting supporters with the three card trick and dice. Five were for pick-pocketing and one for robbery of a purse which contained 14/6d and a return train ticket to Leek!

With the pre-match 'entertainment' concluded, both teams emerged from the changing rooms, with the Bristol players taking to the field first dressed in blue, followed minutes later by United in a change shirt of white, with a red 'V' and a badge showing the red rose of Lancashire which had been presented to the club by comedian George Robey, a staunch supporter of Mangnall's team.

Charlie Roberts won the toss and elected to play with the wind, leaving Bristol City to kick off and from the outset they took the game to United. Gilligan took on the United defence and Hilton's centre caused something of a minor panic. First Roberts and then Stacey cleared the danger and it wasn't until Charlie Roberts was fouled a few minutes later that United managed to gain any real foothold in the Bristol City half. This initial foray came to nothing as Sandy Turnbull, who up until kick-off had been something of a doubt for United due to a suspected broken rib, headed past the post.

Bristol City, however, continued to conduct the flow of the game. Gilligan took a pass from Staniforth in his stride, but he was soon hustled off the ball and the opportunity was gone. Hardy then got the better of Roberts and Bell, before passing to Staniforth, but the Bristol outside right saw his excellent centre wasted by Burton who shot wide of Moger's goal. Charlie Roberts seemed to be at the heart of everything, marshalling his · defence and prompting his forwards and in one of the latter instances, he fed the ball through to Wall, but the winger's shot was brilliantly blocked by City goalkeeper Clay, fisting the ball away to safety whilst on his knees, with Wedlock eventually clearing the immediate danger.

Slowly United clawed their way into the game, with the half back line of Duckworth, Roberts and Bell (immortalised by a Mancunian cigar of the period named 'Ducrobel') beginning to take command. Meredith, grasping at one of the clearances from defence, sent one of his excellent centres into the City goalmouth where Annan completely missed the ball, but fortunately for him, Clay was on hand to make a desperate save. Meredith and Halse on the United right were by now becoming a constant thorn in the side of the Bristol City defence, the former with his constant trickery, the latter with his speed, but despite forcing a number of corners, the initial breakthrough simply failed to materialise. A powerful Duckworth drive hit the side netting, while opportunities also fell to Jimmy and Sandy Turnbull, but both failed to hit the target.

At this point there was a minor off-field distraction when one of the supporters who had decided that the branches of one of the trees which over-looked the ground provided a better advantage point, lost his balance amid the excitement and fell from his perch. Undaunted, it was only a matter of minutes before he was again seen clambering back up to his lofty perch. Bristol City were allowed few opportunities to break, such was the pressure they were now under from United, but on one of the occasions that they did manage to do so Wedlock got the ball wide to Hilton, who in turn drew the United defence a little out of position. From his centre, the unmarked Hardy sent a firm shot towards Moger, but the 'keeper was able to make a superb save, grabbing the ball just below the cross-bar.

With twenty-four minutes gone United once again pushed forward, Roberts urging on his team mates superbly, and an opening was presented to Halse. In the clear, the inside right shot for goal, but was disappointed to see his effort smack the underside of the bar and bounce back into play. However, before any of the City defenders could react, Sandy Turnbull, who had been a severe doubt to play following a recent injury, pounced and drove the ball home from close range. It was a goal in keeping with the play, as other than the few opening minutes, United were clearly the better team. A knock to Meredith held up play for a couple of minutes, but the Welshman was soon restored to fitness and tormenting the Bristol defence as he, along with Duckworth and Halse, more or less strolled through the Robins defence, but the accuracy of United's shooting left a lot to be desired.

Hilton was one of the few Bristol City players who enjoyed much in the way of freedom against the sterling United defence and from one of his forward forages, Staniforth sent a long-range effort narrowly over. Play slackened a little as the interval approached and although Bristol City were now playing the better football, they failed to trouble Moger. Burton and Hardy caused a few minor problems with Staniforth working hard to propel his side forward. On a couple of occasions, he might have beaten Moger, but after moving in from the wing, he elected to pass to a team mate rather than try for goal himself. At the opposite end United still kept Clay in the City goal on his toes, with Sandy Turnbull and George Wall both coming close. With those, and other missed opportunities, United should have been four or five goals in front by the interval, but between the wind blowing several passes astray and their sometimes casual manner, they had to be content with a one goal advantage.

Within five minutes of the re-start Bristol City almost snatched the equaliser. Burton shot for goal, Moger threw himself to the side and saved, with the ball scrambled away to safety. Meredith then came close to doubling United's lead, but play suddenly swung to the opposite end of the field – Hardy found Hilton and from his pinpoint cross, Gilligan headed for goal, Moger flung himself to the right and somehow managed to claw the ball away.

As the second half progressed the game was more evenly balanced, although at times there was considerable foul play, forcing the referee into pulling more than one player to the side for a quick word or two. Meredith came in for more close attention than most and following one rather robust challenge it looked as though the Welshman had seriously damaged his collar-bone. With play moving quickly from end to end, Meredith sought his revenge in his footwork, bamboozling Spear, but Clay saved Sandy Turnbull's effort as he got on the end of the Welshman's cross, while at the other end, Moger was again called upon to keep United in the lead before Hilton shot over.

By now Meredith was running amok and having moved onto a Sandy Turnbull pass and though hampered by Cottle and Spear, he still managed to get a shot at goal, but his low drive was just inches wide. From one of the Welshman's corners after he had toyed with Spear, Jimmy Turnbull headed narrowly over. Opportunities were numerous, but still only a solitary goal separated the two teams.

An injury to Hayes forced the United left back off the field for six minutes and even with United reduced to ten men, Bristol City failed to grasp the advantage. Upon the defender's return, he was limping badly and was forced into an outside right position with Stacey switching flanks and Duckworth and Halse dropping back. Despite this set back and something of a reduction in their attacking options, United, although stretched at times, kept their opponents at bay.

Billy Meredith was by far the outstanding player on view, beating both the City left half and left back with ease, but the tight marking of his team mates failed to see his passes create much in the way of scoring opportunities. Wedlock pushed his front line forward whenever possible, while Hilton twice found himself in an ideal position in front of goal, but on each occasion placed the ball wide, while it was also considered by many that the Bristol City short passing game was not suited to cup-tie football, something that troubled the United defence only on very rare occasions. Had they used their wingmen to more effect, then the result may well have been different.

A Jimmy Turnbull foul presented City with yet another opportunity to level the score but Gilligan shot wide, then twice in as many seconds the United goal had narrow escapes, Halse managing to scramble the ball clear and Moger making something of a lucky save. Both the Turnbulls had opportunities to increase United's lead, but Jimmy, when only a few yards from goal, shot over and then Sandy found himself upended by Annan when almost clean through, the resulting free kick coming to nothing.

But the chance of the second half fell to Bristol City: Stacey made a poor attempt to clear, leaving Hilton with an open goal, but the outside left somehow managed to send his shot wide of the post. Gilligan then shot over after Roberts had been forced to give away a corner and Jimmy Turnbull, once again faced with only Clay to beat, shot over the bar. With five minutes remaining, any attempts made by Bristol City to snatch an equaliser were cleared anywhere by the United defence and with no further scoring, it was the Manchester United supporters who celebrated as the referee signalled the end of the game, with many of those supporters having been seen attempting to move towards the stand side of the ground for a better view of the cup presentation during the closing stages.

In the newspapers of the time, opinions on the final were split. 'Flaneur' in the *Weekly Record* wrote:

> *"The views of Lord Charles Beresford* [a Conservative MP and renowned Admiral] *and of the professional critics who saw the Cup*

Final between Manchester United and Bristol City are somewhat at variance. The critics are generally agreed that even for a Final it was a poor game, and some go so far as to say it was one of the worst specimens seen at the Palace. But Lord Charles said it was one of the finest games that had ever been played in the country, and Dr Macnamara endorsed the great sailor's observations by describing the match as 'a first-class game, played in true, gallant, and sportsmanlike fashion'. Every man to his trade, and Lord Charles and the doctor will no doubt shine more at the Admiralty than as amateur critics of football. Of course, they would be too gallant to say what the professional critics say, but they need not have laid on the butter with a trowel. Perhaps Lord Charles would not agree that 'there were few incidents in the second half worth looking at', perhaps he did not see that thousands of people left the ground a quarter of an hour before the finish; perhaps he failed to observe the excess vigour shown by some of the players, or even the loss of temper by J, Turnbull, when on being given off-side deliberately kicked the ball out of play. All these things are noticed and commented upon by the critics, but Lord Charles Beresford, who was apparently the most popular personality on the ground, said his nice things nicely, and no one was one penny the worse. But the praise was not deserved and apparently only Manchester united and their supporters among the real everyday followers of football appreciated this last Palace Final."

In *The Times*, their correspondent wrote in his

summary of the ninety minutes:

> *"The match was of the kind to which followers of the game have become accustomed since professional clubs have had matters all their own way in the most important competitions. The play, which was extremely fast, with only an occasional sign of slackening, was marked by accuracy of kicking, strong tackling and contrary to custom, heavy charging. In allowing the fair, but robust charge, to go unpunished the referee exercised a wise discretion in the true interests of Association football. As an attraction to the general public the match equalled most final ties, except the one in which the presence of Tottenham Hotspur specially interested London. Nor did the scene differ much from that to which one has grown accustomed at this event. On a very pleasant afternoon the sports arena looked its best, the green turf of playing pitch and trees in the background throwing out in strong relief the thousands of people who came from the west country, and because there was little in the play to cause excitement, Manchester United looked like winners from the start and nothing happened in the nature of a surprise."*

The newspapers of the day devoted countless column inches to United's triumph and in the *Manchester Evening News*, Mangnall confessed that Sandy Turnbull had been a major doubt for the game. *"Sandy played, though the trainer and the specialist and almost everybody agreed that he would not do so. He promised that if he went on the field, he would not come off until the match was over, and he fully redeemed his pledge. We knew he would, and it was the confidence the directors* had in him that induced them at the last moment to give him the opportunity – a decision they cannot now regret."

The United party spent the week-end in London, basking in their glory and taking in the sights of the capital, some quick to say that they would like to live down there. But they were to wave the capital goodbye on the morning of Tuesday April 17th, with Ernest Mangnall leaning out of the train window waving the F. A. Cup as it pulled away from St Pancras Station en-route to the familiar backdrop of Manchester. Upon arrival back in the industrial sprawl of the city, there was no time to return to their homes and put their feet up, as Woolwich Arsenal were waiting at Clayton to play the penultimate game of the First Division season.

An hour before the train was due to arrive at Manchester's Central Station, large crowds had begun to assemble, with barricades having been set up to keep the approach leading to the platform clear. According to the *Manchester Evening News*, *"The great majority wore United colours, and an ice-cream merchant attracted a considerable attention with his huge red and white umbrella and his similarly coloured barrow. Gutter merchants who did a good business with memory cards of Bristol City came in for a good deal of good humoured badinage, while United favours attached to a cardboard representation of the English cup sold like hot cakes."*

By the time United arrived home thousands had gathered around the approach to Central Station, with thousands more in Albert Square. Others avoided the crush by lining the streets between the two to three mile route to Clayton, with an estimated "100,000, mainly men, but including many women, were out on the streets". Upon arrival at the station, the triumphant team were greeted by the band of St Joseph's Industrial School who, as Mangnall appeared, holding the cup aloft, followed by the players, struck up with 'See the Conquering Hero Comes". The crowd then surged forward and some of the players were carried shoulder high to their waggonette.

Although the Town Hall was only a short distance from the station, the team and officials travelled in two horse brakes, with the band in another two, the procession lead by mounted police, Charlie Roberts sitting proudly at the front, clutching the F. A. Cup. Every window space along the route was filled and it was commented that due to the number of workmen present, many must have left their places of employment an hour or two early in order to be there.

Having been greeted by the Lord Mayor, it was off to Clayton, via Deansgate, St. Mary's Gate, Market Street and Oldham Street. In the latter shop assistants threw red roses to the players, while in the "meaner streets of Clayton", the *Manchester Guardian* reported; *"the poorest of the residents had attempted some kind of decoration and the person who moved amongst the throng without flaunting some red and white ribbon would probably have been thought guilty of heresy".*

Such was the time it took to get from Central Station to Clayton, the players just had time to change into their cup colours and take the field, with the directors' box decorated in red and white flowers just for the occasion.

It was little wonder that United lost 4-1 to Arsenal however at full-time it was more or less a repeat of what had gone on a couple of hours or so previously as the United players and officials were due at the Midland Hotel for the official club celebrations. Preceded by supporters carrying torches and also a band, the procession slowly meandered through the streets, which were once again packed with people, the journey taking over two hours and upon arrival at the hotel, there were again large numbers, with the police, mounted and on foot, struggling to keep order. Due to the time it took to make the three mile journey, the seventy people present at the official dinner had their evening cut short due to the lateness of the hour. The party would continue elsewhere, behind closed doors.

If there were hangovers, they had to be out of the system within two days, as there was still one league fixture remaining, at Bradford City and again defeat was suffered, the 1-0 reversal leaving United wallowing in something of an unfamiliar thirteenth place.

On the pitch the season may well have finally come to a close, but while still working under the title of secretary/manager, Ernest Mangnall found little in the way of relaxation. Within a week of having celebrated at Crystal Palace, he was facing what could be considered stronger opposition than Bristol City in the form of the Football League Management Committee, hoping that he could achieve what his players had done – a victory. He was, however, to fail, as despite his reasoning, the Committee decided that he was responsible for fielding an under-strength team on several occasions prior to cup-ties and the club were fined £250. Fortunately, it didn't make much of a dent in the £2,888 the club received for winning the cup.

An appeal was immediately lodged, but this also failed, resulting in the club also losing their £10 deposit, as Mangnall argued that "the club had been seriously handicapped by injuries throughout the season". The *Athletic News*, however, delved into their files for a record of the changes and went to print saying: *"During the first* half of the season, taking the changes from one league game to another, 39 alterations were made. In the second half of the campaign, for an equal number of games, 67 changes were made. The most remarkable fact disclosed was that, during Meredith's suspension the same eleven players turned out for cup-ties, which extended from January 16 to April 24. Accidents are inevitable, but it seemed rather strange that injuries and recoveries should fit in so well with cup ties."

Mangnall had also come head-to-head with some of his players, as the majority had refused to re-sign after being offered the maximum wage and he had reported them to the Football Association, caring little for any backlash from those predominant in the Players Union. He had also placed one of his regular notices in the *Athletic News* seeking players for the next season.

As the warm summer days continued, there was even more heat around Clayton than usual as the United players soon found themselves at odds with those who wielded the power at the club. The Players Union had also locked horns with the Football Association and appeared to be growing in strength. The *Manchester Guardian* carried the following in their July 22nd issue:

> "The decision of the Manchester United players to retain their membership of the Players' Union has caused much perturbation to the management of that club. A director of the club, seen on the matter, said he could not understand the attitude of the men, seeing that (as he thought) they were standing out alone. The men were not only placing themselves but the club in a very awkward position, and at present, with the exception of a few members of the reserve eleven, the only players they had at their command were Stacey, Hayes, Linkson,

Halse, and the new player Bloch [this was in fact Blott] *who was recently secured from Southend. A meeting of the directors of the club will be held to-day to consider the question. The work of preparing the men for the heavy season's programme should be entered upon in less than three weeks' time."*

Despite the dispute and their refusal to re-sign, the United players expressed their loyalty to the club *"and their esteemed president Mr J. H. Davies and to the loyal public that has frequently and generously appreciated their efforts in the field of football."* An article in the *Sheffield Evening Telegraph* on July 22nd added:

"The players desire the public to understand thoroughly that the dispute is not one of wages, or for mastership; it is solely that they are resisting a demand that they relinquish the rights of every worker to associate himself with his fellows, so as to be better able to succour an unfortunate colleague; and that they have refused to surrender their legal rights at the bidding of a body of men who do not contribute a penny-piece to the upkeep of football but who, in many instances, are making considerably more money out of their association with the game than is the highest-paid professional.

"They are eager to play for the United on the 1st of September, but they are debarred from doing so, and they are to be driven out of football because they will not consent to secede from their Union and agree to abject subjection to the whims of the Football Association. The United players, who are fighting the cause of all professional footballers, cannot conceive their fellow-players so base to

contemplate desertion of the Union, and they look forward confidently other players fulfilling their promises to re-join the Union at the opening of the season. They appeal to Trade Unionists to assist them the tight they are making for the principles of Trade Unionism, and they leave it to the public whether they prefer to be entertained by men of their own stamp, or by individuals who have to obey the changing moods of a body which refuses to argue points in dispute, and which demands blind obedience to orders, however unjust or however contradictory.

"Inquiries made among the players, after the meeting, showed that the only players of the Manchester United Cup team who have not announced their intention of retaining their membership of the Players' Union are Stacey, Halse and Hayes. Halse is expected to fall into line with his colleagues. Several members of the reserve eleven have expressed their willingness to follow the lead of their seniors, that the possibility of the United not being able to place a strong eleven in the field has to be faced."

Whether Mangnall, not having played the game at senior level himself, had any sympathy for his players continued to be something for debate, but there must have been some annoyance as he had brought those individuals to the club, built them into a team, and a successful one at that, propelling them to the highest honours in the game, only to be left with mere crumbs and a handful of players with which to plan a season that was drawing closer by the day.

Friday July 23rd was the first pay day for footballers as

agreed by the Football Association, however, in accordance with a resolution passed by the United officials Mangnall did not have many pay slips to fill in or overly much money to place into envelopes as fifteen of his playing staff, who held membership to the Players Union, received nothing. The players, however, were set to bring a test case against the club for the recovery of wages not paid.

The few players who did return to Clayton at the beginning of August found that Mangnall had employed a herd of sheep in order to shorten the grass that had grown considerably on the pitch, while they were also informed by the United manager that the move away from the area to Old Trafford, planned for the beginning of October, would now not happen and it would be perhaps November or December before they would move to pastures new.

Such news was disappointing, as much to Mangnall as it was to the players, who had expected to report to Old Trafford for pre-season training instead of Clayton, where they found not only the sheep, but also the ground in much need of repair; the dressing room doors were hanging from their hinges and riddled with dry rot although a couple of coats of whitewash had been splashed about in the hope of brightening up the place. The United manager was hit by further bad news when several members of the reserve team decided to join their senior counterparts, leaving only five players who had not joined.

For the rebels training was done at Fallowfield, perhaps somewhat strangely under the eye of Fred Bacon the club trainer, while his assistant, J. Nuttall., along with J. Robertson, the reserve team trainer and Mangnall supervised those at Clayton and it was at Fallowfield that a famous photograph materialised. The story behind the photograph was described by Charlie Roberts as follows: *"After training a day or two, a photographer came along to take a photo of us and we willingly obliged him. Whilst the boys were being arranged, I obtained a piece of wood and wrote on it – 'The Outcasts F.C.' and sat down with it in front of me to be photographed. The next day the photograph had a front page of a newspaper, much to our enjoyment, and the disgust of several of our enemies."*

On Saturday August 28th, Mangnall invited the dissenters to a meeting in the Douglas Hotel in regards to a resolution passed by the authorities at a meeting in Birmingham, to *"consider the effect that if a player belonged to the union, he must be treated as a suspended player, and pay a refund."* In reality Mangnall was wasting his time, and probably knew it before he even arrived at the appointed time, and although the meeting was "most harmonious" the twenty-seven players present, including Halse and Hayes who had previously stood back from the on-going saga thus leaving United with no first team players, said that they would like it to be thoroughly understood that they had no grievance whatsoever with the club and that they had always been best friends with the officials and they were quite happy, but they were fighting for what they believed to be a just principle, and therefore they intended to retain their membership of the Players' Union.

As a result of the players continued stance and following a meeting with the United directors, Mangnall had little option but to contact his opposite number at Bradford City and inform him that the First Division fixture between the two clubs, scheduled for Wednesday September 2nd would have to be postponed. His letter to

Mr. Peter O'Rourke read: *"Owing to all our players having re-joined the Players' Union, we regret that is impossible to play our match with you Wednesday next. I take the earliest opportunity of letting you know, so that it shall not inconvenience you."* Similar messages were sent to Mr McHugh of London, the referee appointed for the match and Messrs Alderson and Bowen, the linesmen and the secretary of the Football League.

With the season not even started, United were already playing catch-up. The players would be far from match fit, while Mangnall had the constant worry that the postponement of more games would trigger the football authorities to take action against the club. Although it was far from being United's fault, being unable to field a team to fulfil fixtures would surely see some form of punishment dealt out.

With the new season only twenty-four hours away Mangnall was forced to admit that he had no idea if the second fixture of the season, against Bury at Clayton, would take place, neither could he confirm or deny that if the dispute was not settled that he would be bringing new players to the club, as it had not been discussed at board level. He did say that he thought *"it would be a very risky thing for any club to do, as the people used to seeing first-class fare would not be satisfied with the efforts of a body of men gathered from practically anywhere."*

Not only was Mangnall in a strange and awkward position, it was perhaps even more so for Mr J. J. Bentley, who was not only a United director and also president of the Football League, but he was to add something of a contradictory statement to his manager, saying that United had been *"offered the use of players from various League clubs"*, while another paper added that they had been offered players, but Bentley had refused them!

Then, at the eleventh hour, came a breakthrough, with the Football Association and the Players' Union meeting in Birmingham and agreeing to a settlement which saw all suspensions lifted and arrears in wages to those players who had been suspended being paid. Having been informed, Mangnall hastily re-arranged the Bradford fixture, kicking-off at Clayton at 5.30pm. The United support, upon hearing the news, were still left in the dark as to which players they would see in action.

8: A NEW HOME

DESPITE HASTILY RE-ARRANGING that opening fixture against Bradford City, 12,000 spectators made their way to Clayton for the opening fixture of the 1909-10 season. None who passed through the gates, handing over their sixpences, had any idea as to who they would see in the red shirt, but, although they watched a different eleven emerge on to the pitch than that which brought the curtain down on the previous campaign there were just two changes from the cup-winning side: one being Meredith who had yet to re-sign, the faces were familiar except for new signing Sam Blott at inside-right. After all the uncertainty, the miss-match training and everything else that had blighted the close-season, United got off to the perfect start with two points from a 1-0 victory and had taken to the field amid a great reception from their supporters. Three days later, it was more of the same, Bury being defeated 2-0.

By the time September blended into October, there had been only one defeat (3-2 at Notts County) and after seven games – three wins, three draws and that solitary defeat, United were one of four clubs on nine points, two behind early leaders Everton, but with a game in hand. A 3-2 defeat at the hands of Everton's Merseyside rivals Liverpool threw a spanner in the works, but it was only a temporary setback, as the following five fixtures were all won, including a tempestuous affair against Aston Villa that saw Jimmy Turnbull, along with a Villa player, sent off for "an impromptu bout of fisticuffs".

Columns.	1	2	4	5	
No.	When Married.	Name and Surname.	Age.	Condition.	Rank or Profession.
392	July 25 1906	James Ernest Mangnall	36	Bachelor	Secretary
		Eliza Sharpe Hobson	29	Spinster	—

South Shore   in the County of Lancaster

Residence at the time of Marriage.	Father's Name and Surname.	Rank or Profession of Father.
13 Hill Street	Joseph Mangnall (decᵈ)	Builder
13 Hill Street	Thomas Hobson (decᵈ)	Estate Agent

Details of Ernest's marriage to Eliza in July 1906

The trophies kept on coming for Mangnall's United, here he proudly flourishes the 'Little Tin Idol' the original FA Cup, at a reception outside Manchester town hall, following the 1-0 win over Bristol City.

United's move to the palatial surrounds of Old Trafford was a dramatic contrast to the Bank Street ground that the club had formerly called home. Designed by Archibald Leitch, the original plans for an athletic track were scrapped, as was the original aim for a 100,000 capacity.

GEORGE ROBEY'S TEAM (at Old Trafford, March 6, 1911).—Back Row.—Messrs. J. E. Mangnall, Millward, Rocca, Ashcroft, Bob Crompton, Charlie Thomson, George Livingstone, and Lane. Middle Row.—Bobby Walker, Alf. Pennington, George Robey, Jock Simpson, Bridgett. Front Row.—Sammy Frost, Wedlock, and Hibbert.

Famous music hall star and United fan George Robey organised a charity match at Old Trafford in March 1911 - Mangnall is on the back row far left, Louis Rocca, who went on to recruit Matt Busby in 1945, is third from the left.

The shadow of the Players' Union continued be cast around Clayton and once again the threat of a strike was in the air. Mangnall was caught up in a compromising situation as he had to contact the Football Association and request permission to award Charlie Roberts a benefit match, the centre-half having chosen the fixture against Newcastle United. With the United centre-half being one of those at the forefront of the Players Union, the F. A. were handed, in effect, a smoking bomb. As it was, Roberts still claimed the club owed him a £20 bonus for helping to win the F. A. Cup, but in effect he, along with his team mates, were also owed £28 in lieu of their summer payments.

The Football Association had no qualms in turning down the request, as they felt that to grant privileges and benefits would be to break their own rules, a decision that did not go down well with some of Roberts' team mates and they threatened to strike and not play the Newcastle game and it took a meeting on the morning of the game to avert a postponement. How Mangnall slept at nights during this period is anyone's guess, as he not only had the Players' Union business to contend with, but there was also the on-going work at Old Trafford that had been scheduled to be completed by the end of the year, along with the recent down-turn of results. The Old Trafford move, however, was still some considerable time away and it was hoped that once the dust settled on the Players' Union affair, results would begin to improve. The Football Association were also never far from Mangnall's thoughts as a meeting of the F. A. Council on December 6th had on their agenda '7 - re. Manchester United'. There was nothing more, just the club's name!

According to the much respected, and Manchester

based, *Athletic News*, the Football Association had, for some time:

> "...been diligently but quietly examining the affairs of the Manchester United Club, and the arrangement appertaining to the financial side of the organisation. It is not news that some time ago the governing body was not satisfied that Manchester United was a genuine club -that is to say, that it was formed by the voluntary effort of a number of people resident in the locality of its headquarters, and that there were many shareholders who, with separate interests, had the right to elect directors. The Football Association does not allow the private proprietorship of clubs carried on for the purpose of speculation and profit. To meet the requirements the F.A., two or three years ago, the club was apparently re-modelled. Even so, the F. A. have not been satisfied, and they have been prosecuting inquiries. They demanded the balance-sheet, which was never made public. The share list has been examined. The increases of capital, the alteration of the articles association (without permission), and the issue of debentures for large sums in connection with the building of the new ground at Old Trafford have been matters for consideration, but beyond this it is extremely difficult to discover what has been done.
>
> "The conclusions which have been arrived at have been kept a real secret, but a report, or a minute, to be presented today will probably elucidate the mystery. If Manchester United be private club, masquerading as if there were body of shareholders independent of the proprietor,

it obvious that the foundation must be altered. Rightly or wrongly, there are those who believe that Manchester United were largely responsible for the disturbed atmosphere of football during the last few months, because somebody connected with the management promised the players bonuses for winning the English Cup - promises which were not fulfilled owing to the amnesty. It seems strange that the club can offer inducements of this kind and escape punishment, while a player who asks for money that he is not entitled to, is either fined or suspended. Probably there was doubt about the poor players, but "Not Proven" - the Scottish verdict - has perhaps been returned in connection with Manchester United and their Cup victory. Manchester United have only been in existence a few years, but they have caused talk and some inquiry."

At the meeting, item '7' on the agenda was dealt with quickly, with a committee appointed to look into club affairs. This they did and Mangnall and several of the club directors made their way to London where they appeared behind a locked door in a hearing that lasted for two hours. The meeting did not go overly well from the club's point of view, with a United source saying that they felt that there was "rather erratic behaviour" from certain members of the Committee.

League President Mr. J. J. Bentley, who had recently stood down as a director of Manchester United, [or was his position now untenable?] cast some light on the F.A. v M.U.F.C. situation in an article saying:

"The United Club was originally formed on lines

which were not exactly in keeping with the usage and practice of the Football Association, and when I joined the club I pointed this out. It was then decided that as the president had entailed heavy liabilities, it would be unfair to him to put an end to the club, and I personally guaranteed that the club should be conducted on proper lines i.e., that every penny received should be accounted for. This has been done in its entirety. But, like nearly all other organisations, Manchester United have paid bonuses to players, but unlike most other clubs, these payments have not been made out of the gate receipts, but out of the pocket of a private individual, who, after the amnesty, gave the amount he had so paid to the club officials, and they decided to include it in the balance sheet. The real hitch between the F.A. Commission and the Manchester United arose not owing to the refusal of the club to give details, but because they demanded unconditionally, and, if thought fit, the Commission wanted the right to publish them. This was what Manchester United objected to... I can quite understand the club not desiring their publication, not only their account but as general principle, for, according to the dictionary, 'amnesty' means 'oblivion - wiping out.' Most sportsmen will agree that after the amnesty it would be unfair to reap up matters prior thereto."

As things dragged on many, not just in and around Manchester, were of the opinion that the Football Association had something of a hidden agenda against United, even the decision to hold further meetings and enquiries into the club affairs being held in London rattled more than a few.

Back on the pitch, the five game winning streak back in October, early November, had come to an end with a 3-2 defeat at Blackburn Rovers and this was followed with a 6-2 hammering at home to Nottingham Forest and a 3-0 defeat at Sunderland. That early December defeat in the north-east left United occupying eighth position in the First Division, but only three points behind leaders Blackburn Rovers. Those five defeats to date were looking costly. Even more costly was the new ground at Old Trafford. January 22nd had now been pencilled in as the date for the official opening, with Tottenham Hotspur were the visitors, but it was not to be as further delays pushed the curtains going up until February 19th and the visit of Liverpool.

Meanwhile United continued to struggle; a 2-1 win over Middlesbrough at Ayresome Park being followed by home and away defeats to Sheffield Wednesday (0-3 & 1-4 respectively) before a 2-0 New Years Day win over Bradford City at Bank Street and a 1-1 draw at Gigg Lane, Bury. The club's defence of the FA Cup fell at the first hurdle, Burnley gaining sweet revenge for the previous season's controversies with a 2-0 win at Turf Moor but United were already well out of contention for the league title.

The final game at Bank Street, the club's home for 17 years during which they had been transformed from a glorified works team into a club of national standing, saw a mere 7,000 supporters gather to watch United defeat Tottenham 5-0 with goals from Connor, Hooper, Meredith and a brace from Captain Marvel, Charlie Roberts. A 1-0 defeat at Deepdale only confirmed that the club wouldn't be in need of silver polish at season's end while a stirring 4-3 win up at St James Park against fourth-placed Newcastle only suggested what might have been. The next game would see the club ensconced in a plush new home.

Manchester United's move from inner-city squalor to suburban splendour would prove key to the club's long-term standing. In many ways the club was a century ahead of its rivals, many of whom took until the first decade of the following century before leaving their humble homes amid the terraces for state of the art facilities further afield, for United it would prove to be the making of the club.

For Mangnall the new ground was a tribute to uncounted hours of work that he had put into making Manchester United the club it now was – League Champions and F. A. Cup winners, with players who, when on their game, were of a superior class to their First Division stablemates and now they were to have a home that was up there with the best. However the United secretary was only partly satisfied, as he had looked for an even better stadium than the one designed by Archibald Leitch that now stood on what was once land owned by the Trafford Park Estate and previously used for grazing sheep and cattle. The final design contained no concrete running tack surrounding the playing pitch and the capacity had been reduced from the one time proposed 100,000.

Above all it was the baby of John Henry Davies, but if Mangnall only partly approved of the final design there were others, such as 'Mancunian' in the *Cricket and Football Field* who believed the club's new home was:

> "...*too far from the centre of the city. Nor do I think it would be fair to the present supporters, who have stuck to the club through adversity, to*

*take another ground on the opposite side of the
city to that from which they have always drawn
their patronage, for I don't think they would follow
them."*

How wrong he would eventually prove to be, although
immediately, either side of World War I, there was little
change in average gates at the new ground.

In the *Athletic News* dated March 8th 1909 an article
entitled "A Pen Picture Of The Undertaking" by a
correspondent called 'Tityrus' described the proposed
move to pastures new in great detail and even today it
makes interesting reading, although as you will read one
or two adjustments would be made along the way:

> *"The west of Manchester is destined to be the
> Mecca of sportsmen of that great commercial city. 'To
> the west, to the west' will be the cry of our football
> folks when leaves are falling next autumn. Already
> we have the Lancashire County Cricket ground,
> the polo ground, the curling pond, the Manchester
> Gun Club and numerous other organisations of
> similar character, devoted to pastime and recreation
> to the west of the city.*
>
> *"In September, the Manchester United Football
> Club will fling open its portals and bid all welcome
> in the same locality. The contrast between Clayton
> and the new headquarters of this great football club
> need not be insisted upon. Clayton is situated in
> the very heart of the working-class community, and
> dominated on every hand by about forty huge stacks
> of chimneys belching forth ciminerion smoke and
> malodorous fumes. No doubt there are those who
> feel thankful for a football ground in the vicinity, as*

it does tend to remind the immediate residents that there is some space left where the toiling people can be amused in a healthy and vigorous manner that pleases them. But an ambitious and a vast club like Manchester United appeals to the 800,000 folks of Manchester and Salford, and an area of larger dimensions, with better accommodation for seeing and housing the spectators and situated in a more attractive locality became essential. Hence the decision of the enterprising directors to lay out an enclosure in the west of Manchester. The new ground lies between the Cheshire Lines railway and the Bridgewater Canal, being a little to the left of the Warwick Road North which juts off the Cheshire Road. In other words, walking along the Chester Road towards Stretford, one would turn to the south along Warwick Road for the County cricket ground and exactly opposite to the north for Manchester United football ground.

"The goals in the new arena will be almost west and east, the Stretford goal being the west and the Old Trafford goal to the east. This will give the readers an idea of the exact environment in the locality which is expanding. There will not be any difficulty in reaching the new rendezvous. Electric tramcars already run from Clayton to Old Trafford and from the city direct, by two routes. It is proposed to lay down a circular tramway siding just off Chester Road so that cars can be turned in there, and the passengers having disembarked, the cars can run round the western end of the circle and return to Manchester for more freight.

"There is here a bridge over the Cheshire

Lines railway which is to be widened so as to cope with the traffic, while further north on the other side of the ground it is intended to throw a bridge over the canal. But apart from those approaches we understand that the Cheshire Lines committee will open a special station within two or three minutes' walk of the western end of this home of sport, so that people can step off the train into the immediate precincts. With such conveniences as these there should never be any difficulty in getting to the place or away from it.

"The Manchester United club have resolved to lay out and equip a huge ground wholly and solely dedicated to football. There will be a running or cycling track around the grass, and for football alone there will be no better enclosure in England. It is to accommodate 100,000 people and if the greatest matches of the day are not in turn decided to Manchester we shall be surprised, especially as the club is not frightened to expend £30,000 on the undertaking.

"When sightseers cross over the railway bridge, they will find themselves in the midst of a clear space which will serve as a gathering ground one hundred and twenty feet broad for spectators and there need not be congestion in gaining access to any portion. With this ground laid out for football alone, the sightseers are brought as near as possible to the playing portion.

"The ground will be rectangle in shape with the corners rounded and it is designed so that everybody will be able to see. The pitch for the game will be excavated to a depth of nine feet from the

ground level so that the boundary or containing wall which is to surround the whole place will only be thirty feet high. There are numerous and spacious exits round the ground. Ingress will be easy and it is estimated that a full ground can be emptied in five minutes.

"Now let us assume that the ordinary spectator has passed through the turnstile. He will find himself in a passage twenty feet broad, which girdles the whole area. From this, access can be obtained from any portion of the popular terracing, which is virtually divided into three sections. There will be one hundred steps of terracing constructed on a special plan and a nicely judged gradient with of course Leitch's patent crush barriers. The lower portion of this terracing is solid ground, the next higher is formed by the excavated earth and the last and highest is built entirely of ferro-concrete, which is as hard as rock and non-flammable.

"With his practical experience of all the best grounds in these islands, Mr Archibald Leitch M. I. M. E. of Manchester, who has been the only designer, has endeavoured to cope with these problems. There seems every reason to believe that he has solved it.

"Now, from this twenty foot passage which will of course afford protection from rain until it absolutely necessary to go into the arena, the herds of human beings can melt away at will. Right in front of the visitor, whichever entrance they take, will be a flight of very broad but easy stairs, which end in a wide opening or mouth, sixty feet wide and split into three sections.

"The stream of sightseers mounting these stairs and reaching the opening find themselves rather above the middle of the terracing which they can spread themselves at will. We can picture these great mouths vomiting thousands upon thousands human beings onto this glorious amphitheatre. The advantage of each mouth is its central position. But if the spectator wishes to go right on top of the terracing, any tier above sixteenth, he will take another wide staircase which hugs the inside of the boundary wall and lands him on the top of forty tiers of concrete, resting on foundations of the same material, the space underneath being utilised for refreshment rooms and other conveniences.

"Means are provided for transferring from one portion of the ground to another, but it is expected that in a ground devised on this plan, with so many conveniences for reaching the particular position that the spectator desires, there will be little call for transfers and certainly not to the same extent as on other enclosures.

"The accommodation will, as said, provide for 100,000 people. Of these, 12,000 will be seated in the grandstand and 24,000 standing under steel and slated roofs, so that together there will be room for 36,000 folk under cover and 64,000 in the open, divided between the two arcs of a circle and the mammoth terracing behind each goal. The roofed part for the populace will be on the southern side and will have wide open ends with overhanging eaves so that no portion of this erection will obstruct the view of those who are not fortunate enough to secure its shelter on an inclement day.

"The special feature of the grandstand compared with similar erections is that there will not be a paddock in front of it. The spectators will be seated from the barricade round the pitch direct to the back of the stand, in fifty tiers. These fifty tiers are again divided into three sections, the lower, the middle and the highest. Spectators desiring to be comfortable in the grandstand will enter from the turnstiles facing the mouth of Chester Road. They are especially reserved for grandstand visitors only and there they can only obtain tickets for any part of the stand.

"Entering there, the spectator will find themselves in a corridor along which run tea rooms, referee apartments, the player's facilities, a gym, billiard room and laundry. All of which are to be fitted up in the most modern manner. From this central corridor, there are means of access to three sections of the grandstand. The lowest or front portion will be approached by a number of passages on the ground floor. To the middle or central portion there are stairs which run practically the whole length of the stand. The highest part is to be gained by means of a distributing passage which is as long as the stand and twenty feet broad. Stairs lead from this to the loftiest section. Thus, it will be seen that the structure is designed in such a manner that each person will be able to get to his seat with the least discomfort to himself and the minimum inconvenience to his neighbours, because there is a separate means of ingress to each section of the stand.

"The man who wishes to go to the top of the

stand has not to disturb those sitting in the lower rungs and this applies to each portion for every detail has been carefully thought out, both by Mr Leitch the mastermind and Messers Bramfield and Smith of Manchester who were responsible for the extensions and improvements at the Clayton ground, the present home of Manchester United F. C.

"Altogether, the entire area of the new home of Manchester United will be sixteen acres. The outward circumference of the ground will be about 2000 feet. The ground will be six hundred and thirty feet long and five hundred and ten feet broad, with the width of the terracing being one hundred and twenty feet. This is a palatial ground which will challenge comparison with any in Great Britain. The executives of the club are to be congratulated on their spirited policy which no doubt will be met with reward from the football public."

On February 16th, an official inspection of the ground was made by Ernest Mangnall, J. H. Davies and his directors, accompanied by a large number of inquisitive journalists. One of which represented the *Manchester Evening News*:

"There is accommodation for over 40,000 people on the six-penny side and the covered stand will hold nearly 13,000. The entire portion [of the stand] is filled with tip up chairs, covered with plush and these have been so arranged that at the close of a match, the coverings can be removed and stocked in a room adjoining, until required again. Behind these are arranged the seats for directors and visiting officials.

> *"Underneath the stands there is the boardroom,
> secretary's office, player's recreation rooms,
> gymnasium, dressing rooms and an elaborate series
> of baths. The Manchester and Salford Corporation
> are completing arrangements for carrying the
> spectators to the ground for the opening match and
> cars will also run on many Manchester routes. In
> addition, the cricket ground station will be opened.
> The task is so far advanced."*

The task may well have been far advanced, thanks to Humphrey's the Knightsbridge builders, but they had to continually pester Mangnall over a period of time in order to extract payment for the work that they had done. It actually got to the stage that Humphrey's became so disappointed with the club that a solicitor was employed and for a number of years, the club were paying around one third of their gate receipts to the builder. Humphrey's were certainly not the only ones who had to wait on money owed as the more local Ellison's, the Salford turnstile manufacturers, whose work could be found at countless venues, had to wait seven months before a cheque popped through their letter-box. Had Mangnall, Davies and his fellow directors bitten off more than they could chew?

The arrival of Liverpool for the ground's first game on Saturday February 19th saw the prospect of thousands of people converging on the (still quite rural) area. Local businesses quickly sprung up to take advantage of this influx of trade. One local who was particularly keen in this regard was Mr J. H. Hargreaves, the landlord of the nearby Dog and Partridge Hotel who attempted to obtain a licence to sell alcohol at the new ground.

"Football and Drink" proclaimed the headline of an

article in the *Manchester Evening News* of February 17th, with *"Licence Sought for Manchester United New Ground. Application Refused."* The article read:

> *"At Manchester County Police Court this morning, before Mr J. M. Yates KC, an application was made by Mr J. H. Hargreaves of the Dog and Partridge Hotel, for an occasional licence to sell drink at the new ground. The applicant explained that he wanted permission to sell at five bars on the ground between 3pm and 6pm. Mr Yates: 'They refuse to grant applications in other large towns. If you want anything of the sort, you must apply at the council meeting of licensing justices. It is a matter for them not me. The football public must be a curious lot, if they cannot watch for two hours without having a drink.'*

The stipendiary refused the application, so the landlord of the Dog and Partridge had to be content with the supporters passing through his doors prior to the game and then perhaps returning to debate the afternoon's entertainment after the final whistle."

As kick off time approached on that momentous Saturday afternoon it was not easy to estimate the actual attendance but outside, both around the ground and on the approach roads it was quite obvious that both the gatemen at the turnstiles and the Manchester Tramways were having difficulty in coping with the vast crowds. Today the record books give an attendance at a rounded up 45,000, but it is to be believed that around 5,000 more managed to gain illegal entry by various means, including a small unfinished window fanlight. So, the lush green turf, with its vivid white line markings, looked immaculate as the sun shone down, with the red and white quartered corner flags fluttering in the afternoon breeze. The surroundings were all something of a dream for however many were indeed present, but they were soon brought back down to reality with a bump, as Liverpool spoiled the party winning 4-3, the visitors fighting back from 2-0 down. It had all started so well as within fifteen minutes United were in front, Sandy Turnbull christening the new ground by latching onto a Dick Duckworth free kick to head the ball firmly past Hardy in the Liverpool goal and immediately make himself for future quiz questions. Or, as the correspondent from the Manchester Guardian seen it - *"Duckworth took a free kick … and skillfully dropped the ball some 10 yards or more from the goal-mouth. A. Turnbull rushed in with lowered head. The ball was within a foot or two of the ground by the time he got it but he met it with that extra-durable head of his and drove it hard into the goal."* A few minutes later, it was 2-0, Homer following through on a Harold Halse shot that the Liverpool goalkeeper failed to hold. It was the perfect start to life at the new venue.

United managed to maintain their advantage until the interval, but after the re-start the visitors began to regain some of the play, keeping Stacey and Hayes, the two United full backs, well occupied. Their pressure soon paid off and they pulled a goal back through outside right Goddard, his shot going in off the underside of the cross bar. The two goal advantage, however, was soon re-established, when George Wall scored with a fine shot from an oblique angle, blasting the ball past two defenders before it beat Hardy at his left hand post. Despite this further setback, the white shirted Liverpool players refused to give in and their resilience was rewarded as they began to get the better of the United defence. Goddard, with his second of the afternoon, soon made it 3-2. Stewart then not only equalized, but then a few minutes later scored what was to be the winner, as rain began to fall on the now subdued home spectators. It was certainly not the best of starts, but with the surroundings just as unfamiliar to the United players as they were to the visitors, it was not what could have been considered a shock defeat.

'Jacques', a correspondent in the *Athletic News* wrote: "*Manchester United are a curious side. A week ago, they defeated Newcastle United after being three goals to the bad at the interval, and now they open the finest ground in the country, before at least 45,000 people, by suffering defeat by four goals to three, after leading at the interval by two goals to none, and also leading midway through the second half by three goals to one.*" He went on: "*In many respects, it was an extraordinary match. The turf, which had been especially laid, and which looked a fit venue for a tennis tournament, was tremendously fast and, contrary to expectation, this proved more in favour of Liverpool.*"

Having got the initial fixture out of the way, things could now only become easier in the day to day running of the club. There was still a considerable amount of work to be done, but it was not long before the new stadium was being acknowledged as one of the best, if not the best in the country but even the new ground did not escape the scrutiny of the Football Association, as newspapers of Thursday March 23rd carried the latest episode in their ongoing "Manchester United Inquiry" saga:

> "*The Commission of Inquiry into the affairs of the Manchester United Football Club recommended to yesterday's meeting of the Football Association Council that the ground at Old Trafford should be valued by an independent valuer. The provision for payment of £740 a year rent for the 14 acres of no*

*use to the club until the Manchester Brewery Co.
required it themselves, and to leave the stands, etc.,
which cost £800 for the Brewery Co., on payment
of £100, is, the Commission think, unreasonable.
The terms of lease and purchase require to be
rearranged before the public are asked to subscribe
capital.*

*"The club is now, says the report, practically
Mr Davies's, managed by him and his nominees.
The Commission think that the management has
been extravagant. No attempt has been made to
reduce the liabilities to Mr Davies, so that the club
could be put on the usual basis of management
and control in pursuance of undertaking given in
August, 1901. The public should not be asked to
contribute capital to meet present liabilities beyond
the present assets, which should be valued by an
independent valuer, and approved by the F.A. If
there any deficiency this should be discharged by the
present management. The club should be properly
constituted and managed in accordance with the
requirements the F.A. Lord Kinnaird moved the
adoption of the report, which was carried, and
Manchester United Club was ordered to comply
with the recommendations without delay, and pay
the whole of the expenses incidental sittings of the
Commission."*

United's rollercoaster form continued: an Aston Villa
victory was perhaps of no surprise as United were forced
into three changes and were among the leaders in the
First Division, but the final 7-1 scoreline that shunted
them above Notts County, who had lost 2-0 at home

to Bristol City that same afternoon sent something of a shockwave through the league. United were now eighth, yet only eight points adrift. 40,000 watched the club's first ever win at Old Trafford (1-0 over Sheffield United on 5th March 1910) followed by a goalless draw away at Arsenal before back-to-back wins over Bolton (5-0) and Bristol (2-1). A 1-1 draw at Stamford Bridge and a 2-1 defeat at Ashton Gate to Bristol City closed out March.

Despite their feelings in regards to the club, the Football Association had no qualms about asking Old Trafford to host the F. A. Cup semi-final replay between Everton and Barnsley, but with certain sections of the ground still incomplete, ticket applications had to go to Mangnall at his Clayton office rather than the new ground, despite this a Thursday afternoon crowd of 55,000 saw Barnsley prevail 3-0.

In three of the opening four games of that 1909-10 season, Jimmy Turnbull's goals had been vital in earning United both points, but those had dried up and his appearances became limited, so much so that following a dispute with Mangnall he was placed on the transfer list in January and looked to be heading back north of the border to join Heart of Midlothian. Then, in early March, when Turnbull had still not appeared in a United line-up, it was announced that he had been suspended *sine-die* by the club, with no love lost between player and officials. Then, a matter of days after that decision, the suspension was removed and Turnbull was back in the first team line-up where he remained long enough to receive a benefit. It made for a strange and still unexplained episode.

The end of March brought an end to the Football Association's enquiry into the club's affairs, with the final report filling seven quarto pages, tracing the history of the club, initial share allocation and much more. The balance sheet of 1909 had shown a figure in excess of £17,000 but had not included a detailed account of expenses for T. Cook & Son for the continental tour and £293 for training at Sandiway. The auditor, a Mr. Thomas Hindle, also pointed out that a sum of £614 7s 10d, paid for rent of the ground should have gone under revenue and not placed to capital. No sum had gone through the accounts for rent accrued due on the Stretford Ground between January 1st 1909 and April 30th. It was estimated that a sum of £400 should have been showing. A sum of £7229 6s 5d had been charged to the profit and loss account and credited to Mr Davies. This, in the opinion of the auditor, was for payments in violation of the rules of the Football Association, including about £700 interest made by Mr Davies between May 1903 and March 1909. The financial doings of Mr Davies were also gone into with a fine toothcomb and the Commission were not satisfied in regards to payments made to two individuals, one of whom was Billy Meredith.

No AGM, as required by the Companies Act, had been held in the previous year, nor had any return made to the Registrar of Joint Stock Companies, omissions that rendered the company and every officer liable to heavy penalties. The club articles of association had also been altered without the sanction of the F. A. and under these, Debentures had been issued to the contractors who were erecting a new stand.

As a result of the enquiry, an independent valuer had to be obtained so that a fair rental for the ten acres that the new ground stood on, due to the relationship between the club and Mr Davies's brewery company. The annual rent of £740 and the undertaking to leave at the expiration of the lease the stands and buildings which had been erected by the club at a cost of over £18,000 upon payment by the brewery company of £100, were both considered unreasonable. The terms of the lease and purchase were also required to be arranged before the general public were asked to submit capital.

The United management were considered "extravagant" and the club were advised to become *"properly constituted and managed in accordance with the requirements of the F.A."* and were told to *"comply with the recommendations without delay, and to pay the expenses incident to the Commission."*

Ernest Mangnall had much work to do, while others were of the opinion that United had got off lightly. One newspaper adding – *"This sequel is rather different to the punishment inflicted upon Manchester City a few years ago as the direct outcome of which Manchester United built up the team that won the Cup last season."* Mangnall, as club secretary, might well have found fingers pointed in his direction, as he would have been heavily involved in all the affairs of the club and who is to say that had the F.A. Commission come down like a ton of bricks on United that the club officials could have faced sanctions.

9: Champions Again

THE 1909-10 SEASON had barely been confined to the record books, the dust from the Football Association enquiry still showing in traces around the Trafford Park area of Manchester, when Ernest Mangnall pulled open his desk drawer, lifted out his well thumbed cheque book, scribbled down a number of figures and popped it into the post to Nottingham Forest in return for their centre-forward Enoch 'Knocker' West. Jimmy Turnbull was going, as he had refused to re-sign and in any case it well known that he was always going to at the end of the season, so the centre-forward position required filling and securing West was a notable piece of work for an individual whose style was described in one newspaper as "resolute, forceful and thrusting" and in another the picture was painted of a "strong, dashing forward, a prolific goal scorer with a too-pronounced tendency towards individualism."

In signing West, Mangnall had to be certain that everything was done by the book and not simply because of the recent enquiry but due to the fact that the transfer was the first of a prominent individual under the new transfer ruling whereby in lieu of a 'benefit', a player was entitled to a share of the fee paid, according to his length of service. Knowing this, along with the fact that Forest were not the richest of League clubs and the additional fact that they would have to have paid West a benefit had he stayed at the club, the United manager/secretary made his move. However, unbeknown to Mangnall at the time, West was also bringing more than just his football boots and a suitcase with him on the train up from the Midlands...

Few were surprised at Mangnall's ability to secure the signature of a player of West's calibre as his standing in football was up there with the best, and the *Cricket and Football Field* of July 9th 1910 asserted that the mastermind behind this signing was also the brain behind United's continued rise, "*One of the best-known figures in connection with present day football management is Mr J. E. Mangnall, the able secretary of the Manchester United Club. Mr Mangnall ranks as one of the all-round school of sportsmen and sports organizers*". After relating his interest in cycling and his cross-country running achievements, it finished with – "*His present appointment with the Manchester United Club began on January 8th 1903, at the time when the club were located among the humble and lowly of the land. All the Mancunians' triumphs, we may add, have dated since Mr Mangnall's advent in Cottonopolis.*"

But not all of Mangnall's transfer dealings went quite so smoothly as the deal for West nor was his judgement infallible. Having signed Leslie Hofton from Glossop for an agreed fee of £1,000 and sent a 'bill' for that amount, it was refused at the bank forcing the Glossop club to contact Mangnall and ask him to have the 'bill' backed by J. H. Davies. The club president refused to do so and denied any responsibility in the matter. Mangnall then returned to Glossop and said that he was not going to pay the £1,000, as it had been discovered that Hofton was "unsound". Akin to a tennis match, Glossop rallied with the fact that they had re-signed Hofton in April on wages of £4 per week and that it was Mangnall who had approached them for the player. Hofton had spent the summer playing cricket, as a fast bowler, and had Glossop said there was no reason to suspect he had any medical condition.

Everything was placed in the hands of a Commission and it decided that the Glossop officials had transferred the player in good faith and that the United officials had not taken sufficient precautions to discover the condition of the player. They added that Mr Davies had done the right thing in refusing to have anything to do with the matter, as it was a club affair. United were told to forward an acceptable 'bill' or pay Glossop £1,000 within fourteen days. They were also ordered to pay the expenses of the Commission and those of the Glossop representatives. The transfer was later completed, Hofton undergoing an operation, the 'bill' in question being dropped and United paying Glossop £1,000 in four £250 instalments. Not that they didn't have £1,000 sitting in the bank!

The club's move across Manchester had obviously been an expensive one, but attendances had increased, as J. H. Davies was quick to point out when he entertained the men of the press in the boardroom prior to the United trial match at Old Trafford in August 1910, mentioning that the gates in the second half of the previous season had averaged almost three times as much as in the first half at Bank Street. Mangnall was a notable absentee from the luncheon as he had gone on what was described as a "missionary expedition", but his club president was to add that he was *"never so confident in the team as at present, and was looking forward to one of the best seasons the club had ever had, for the players were now more settled than at this time last year, and good enough to win the highest honours."* Having not raised enough for charity in that trial match, a second was hastily arranged in order to do so.

For the fourth season in a row the name Turnbull was prominent among the early season goal scorers. Jimmy had taken the honours in 1908-09 and 1909-10, with ten in the opening five fixtures of the former and four from four in the latter, while it was Sandy in 1907-08 with eight in the first half dozen games who took the honours. With Jimmy out of the picture, it was Sandy once more who did the necessary, scoring four in the first five fixtures of 1910-11 to leave United in second spot, a point behind early leaders Sunderland. The season had kicked-off with a 2-1 win in London against Arsenal, with the only reversal in the opening nine fixtures coming against Nottingham Forest by the odd goal in three. Enoch West had proved to be an instant hit, scoring on his debut against Arsenal and adding a further five in the eight games that followed. Mangnall had an even bigger smile on his face when it came to counting the afternoon's takings as the Old Trafford turnstiles clicked merrily away. Forgetting the 45,000 or more who had witnessed that first Old Trafford fixture against Liverpool, the first real test of the ground's ability to cope with a vast number of spectators and Mangnall's ability to ensure that everything ran smoothly on a match day with a near capacity crowd came on September 17th 1910 when Manchester City travelled across town for their first Old Trafford visit, having been promoted as Second Division champions at the end of the previous season. Once again, figures for that afternoon's attendance vary from 60,000 down to 55,000 – a figure accredited to Mangnall as he mentioned that some 52,000 paid for admission and that gate receipts were around £1,700 and overall the attendance was over 55,000 "with room for several thousand more."

Mangnall had come under fire following the first

home fixture of the season against Blackburn Rovers when many complained about there not being enough turnstiles open, but for the visit of City he was free from complaint as 'Mancunian' of the *Cricket and Football Field* had wandered around the ground prior to kick-off and counted over fifty turnstiles open. Of the match in general he added, *"Naturally the United camp was a merry one, for did they not gather all the plums, including a record gate and two valuable points, and did not their team give such a display as to prove conclusively that, for the present at least, they are undoubtedly Manchester's premier team? That they deserved to win no one could possibly deny, for they played the better football, and always seemed to have a 'hit up their sleeve' in case of emergencies."*

As the season got into its stride Mangnall's men found their feet and were to lose only two more games before November was out, 2-1 at home to Middlesbrough and 3-2 against Liverpool on Merseyside while two more were drawn. But those two points, plus the five victories over the course of October and November were still not enough to propel United to the top of the division. They remained two points adrift of Sunderland, having played the same number of games and level on points with Aston Villa who had played a game less. United took every ninety minutes in their stride and on their day had the beating of whoever came their way, but one opponent they could never quite shake was the Football Association Commission who, like a top class defender, kept a wary eye on events down Old Trafford way. Perhaps even more so since the recent investigations.

★

On October 1st, the Scottish *Daily Record* carried the following:

"MANCHESTER UNITED F.C. - CONTROLLING INFLUENCE OF DAVIES TO CEASE. Since the decision of the Council of the English F.A. on Manchester United F.C.'s affairs the Commission have been in communication with the club, and made the following further recommendations: — The present lease from the Manchester Brewery Co. Ltd. to be cancelled, it being admitted that the brewery company purchased the land at Old Trafford as the agents for and on behalf of the club; the club shall be liable for the purchase money, and payment be secured by a mortgage to the brewery company to secure the amount of purchase money and interest at 3 per cent, the Council having already decided that the public should not be asked to contribute the capital to meet the present liabilities beyond the value of the present assets.

"The Commission report that on April 30 the assets and liabilities were:— Assets - Purchase money of land at Old Trafford. £26,497: expenditure on stands, etc.. £35,749 6s 1d; sundries, £328 14s 6d; Total assets - £62,575 0s 7d. Liabilities — Capital, £160; bank. £7076 0s 6d; sundry creditors, £3923 14s 11d; Manchester Brewery Co. for purchase and interest. £27,430 8s 2d; Humphrys Ltd.. stands. etc., £18,137 9s; Mr. J. H. Davies. advances and interest advanced in breach of rules as previously reported, £11,345 19s 11d. Total liabilities, £68,073 126 6d.

"The foregoing statement shows liabilities

of £5,499 11s 11d exceeding the assets, but considerable sums have been paid by the club in the acquisition of players, who are still with the club, and the Commission are of the opinion that the deficiency may be considered as fully met by the value of those players to the club.

"The Commission therefore recommend the Council to approve a scheme for the proper constitution and management of the club upon the basis of the above statement of assets and liabilities, with the addition of the expenditure since April 30 1910. and that the club be required to take such proceedings as may be necessary to carry the same into effect by raising capital and obtaining members commensurate with the status of the club, so that the present controlling influence of Mr. Davies, shall cease."

While Mangnall remained more or less in the background at United and was more than happy to remain so, one or two of his charges were far from shy at coming forward, possibly due to the fact that a couple pound notes might find their way into the pocket on the back of one or two stories. November 1910 saw two of his players put pen to paper, or at least give interviews to certain newspapers, neither revealing anything about their manager, but, certainly in the case of Charlie Roberts, revealing some interesting titbits of life at the club in those distant days. In the *Midland Mail*, under the heading of 'Players' Peculiarities', Roberts spoke of how Billy Meredith played with his toothpick firmly clenched between his teeth, but revealed that *"a United director would bring a new quill every match-day, and it is often amusing to see curio-hunters – boys and very often men – waiting for Meredith after the match to persuade him to let them have the quill used that day."* He spoke of a United team mate who had eleven corks and who would arrange them on a table and play out the game that was to take place the following day. When they won the cup, the player in question named the score and the scorer in the first round tie and so had to do likewise prior to each subsequent round. More revealing was the fact that at Clayton, each player had their own numbered dressing room.

Sandy Turnbull, on the other hand, told of why he had become a footballer, saying that he "loved football and I love the life of fitness, clean living and the athlete's outdoor life." Although, like Roberts, he did not mention Mangnall by name, but he spoke at length about training and how it gave a lad *"a bigger and a better outlook in life"*, adding that a player's chief aim must be to train upon scientific lines, perhaps it's all according to your director's ideas, but there must be no slacking. Elsewhere he mentions *"the special training, the week-end and perhaps, mid-week battle royal, the flattery of well-meaning friends if you are successful and the woes expressed if you are not."* As I said, there is no mention of Ernest Mangnall, but he is in there between the lines.

January 1911 saw the F. A. Cup make its appearance on the fixture lists, with United drawn away to Blackpool. As he lived in the area Mangnall was well aware of the financial problems that enveloped the seaside club and no sooner had the names of the clubs been drawn out of the hat than he was in touch with the Blackpool directors asking them if they would be prepared to move the tie to Old Trafford. "We will give you between £300 and £350 or half of the gate money" was the United secretary's offer. Following much discussion, it was agreed that Blackpool would receive a guarantee of £600 and sixty per cent of gate receipts over £900.

Generous United may have been but they had been equally generous in their December league fixtures, losing three out of the seven and failing to score in any of that trio. A 2-0 victory over leaders Aston Villa on December 17th, coupled with second placed Sunderland dropping a point against Notts County, left United level at the top on twenty-four points with their two title challengers. Seven days later Sunderland were beaten 2-1 at Roker Park propelling them into top spot as Villa had drawn with Liverpool. The emphatic 5-0 hammering of Woolwich Arsenal on Boxing Day kept them in pole position, a point in front of Villa, who had a game in hand, and two ahead of Sunderland. Yet before the bells chimed in the new year United should have consolidated their position, but consecutive 1-0 defeats, at Bradford City and Blackburn Rovers allowed Villa back into the mix and the pair were level on twenty-eight points, Sunderland trailing the leaders by two points.

No sooner had January appeared on the calendar than new recruits were added to the payroll with the *Athletic News* of January 2nd 1911 reporting: *"Mr. Ernest Mangnall of Manchester United is one of the most far seeing, as well as one of the most successful, of club managers. He does not wait for a weakness to develop in the team he controls before he acts. He is ever building and on Saturday he strengthened the resources of his club by securing the transfer of Victor McConnell, the centre half back, from Cliftonville, and Hamill, the inside-right from Belfast Celtic. Mangnall is to be congratulated on his enterprise."* Only Hamill was to make any sort of impression over the water.

Two days into the New Year it was back to winning

ways with a 1-0 victory over Bradford City at Old Trafford. Nottingham Forest were then beaten 4-2, again at home, before Blackpool arrived to fulfil their F.A. Cup engagement, with the Seasiders putting up a spirited fight, losing by the odd goal in three, but content in knowing that they had at least gained a victory financially. A week after that cup victory, a 1-1 draw against neighbours City at Hyde Road saw United edge three points clear at the top but they had played two games more than second placed Aston Villa whose game at Arsenal that same afternoon had been abandoned. Another draw followed, 2-2 at third place Everton, allowing Villa to close the gap. Only four points separated the top four clubs.

The draw for round two of the cup wasn't as kind to Mangnall as it might have been, there would be no need to bribe the opposition with a nice cheque in order to persuade them to come and play in Manchester as United were drawn at home, but such an idea would never have materialised as the opposition were fellow giants of the age, Aston Villa. A victory against the championship challengers would be more than welcome and might just knock the Midland side off their stride for a week or two. Mangnall, as he had prior to the previous round, took his players to Buxton for a few days, as the forthcoming tie grabbed the imagination of the football loving Mancunian public and on the day of the game, the Old Trafford turnstiles went into overdrive with 65,101 squeezing inside, paying receipts of £2,464, a record for any game played in the city up until that date.

Resplendent in red and white striped shirts, it was the grit and determination of Duckworth, Roberts and Bell in the United half-back line who dominated the ninety minutes. West and Wall missed opportunities to open the scoring, as did Hampton for Villa, but it was Wall who gave United the advantage from a corner kick, with Halse adding a second before half-time. Villa managed to grab what was to prove a consolation towards the end, but there was never going to be a fight back nor a replay to decide the outcome. Between that second round victory and the third round tie against West Ham United at Upton Park, United consolidated their position at the top of the table with victories over Bristol City [3-1] and Newcastle United [1-0]. The gap at the top was now three points and Villa still had two games in hand. Many were of the opinion that Mangnall's men were heading to the Cup Final again, but no-one would put their cards on the table in regards the league title.

The Southern League was not too far below the level of the Football League First Division and it was believed that many of the clubs at that level would feel comfortable going head-to-head with any club within the top flight. West Ham's chairman was certainly one of those who felt his team had the ideal players to combat United's threat from their wide men. The West Ham manager, Mr. E. S. King, meanwhile was of the opinion that Mangnall's team were "possibly the best team in the world". Quite a statement!

While at Whitley Bay prior to the fixture against Newcastle United, Mangnall was asked about the forthcoming cup-tie and was somewhat reluctant to be drawn into a discussion and would only say: *"We know our men will do their utmost, and we have great confidence in them."* If the United manager hand any worries, it was being without goalkeeper Harry Moger, who would miss the remainder of the season due to having an operation on his leg.

It took just seventeen minutes for West Ham to take the lead, through Shea, but five minutes later the two teams were level when Turnbull converted from a Meredith corner. In the second half, play flowed from end to end, with both teams missing good scoring opportunities and as the minutes ticked away it looked as though the match was going to a replay. Then, with two minutes remaining, Whiteman centred and Caldwell put the ball beyond the reach of Edmonds and West Ham marched into round four. However defeat didn't end Mangnall or United's interest in the F. A. Cup, as the final played at Crystal Palace on April 22nd between Newcastle United and Bradford City was drawn 0-0 and the replay was scheduled for Old Trafford four days later, putting the club secretary and staff under immediate pressure. Considering the short period of time that they had the task at hand was only accomplished with an "all night sitting" at Old Trafford.

Speaking to the *Manchester Courier* on the eve of the showpiece replay Mangnall stated that: *"the whole of the 4,500 reserved 5s. seats had been disposed of, and even then, there were applications pouring into the office by letter and telegram. At first 2,000 seats were reserved, but such was the demand that it had been decided to increase the number to 3,000, and subsequently to 4,500. The whole of the grand stand chairs, together with large blocks either side, have been turned into 5s. seats. There will still be extensive accommodation at the back the stands for the 2s. spectator and a big block at one end of the stand will available for the 2s. 6d. man." Mangnall also stated that applications had come from such far off places as Aberdeen, Edinburgh, Belfast, and South Wales."* He went on to add: *"The Bradford City club had sent in order for 300 more 5s. tickets, making 600 in all, for all of which, of course, they pay and at a rough estimate there would be accommodation for 50,000 people at 1s."*

There was also an enormous application for Press tickets, and the Manchester Press Committee, whose usefulness Mr. Mangnall spoke of in warm terms, were allocated something like one hundred tickets for working journalists. The *Courier* went on to add:

> *"The fact that Post Office officials have decided to place a telegraph office on the ground will be the greatest service for this army of Pressmen. A room on the ground floor has been set apart for this purpose, where messages will be received for conveyance at the expense of the Post Office to the head telegraph office in the city. This will be a great boon to visiting Pressmen, who, on the occasion of the replayed semi-final tie between Barnsley and Everton [the previous season], had to engage the services of taxi cabs to get their messages from Old Trafford to Manchester. The public may also make use of these facilities, and for their guidance it may be stated, that the office is situated just near the main entrance to the stand.*
>
> *"It was at first suggested that the telegraph office at the County Cricket ground, close at hand, should be opened for the occasion, but the Post Office authorities found that this would not be possible owing to a clause in the agreement, which prohibits the cricket ground telegraph service being used for other matters. It is expected that next season a permanent telegraph service will be installed at the United ground, which appears to be destined to have many more great matches played"*

Mangnall added: *"Owing to the very large number people who will have to be conducted to their seats it is absolutely imperative that holders of reserved tickets should be at the ground in good time. Everything possible will done to see that ticket-holders are conducted to their seats, and late comers will have only themselves blame if they do not receive the same attention as those who have taken the wiser course of being at the scene in good time. A special staff will be on duty to look after the reserve ticket holders, and all round the ground special placards have been issued directing the public to the various entrances and stating the prices."*

The United secretary's job was not an easy one as every aspect of the final fell onto his desk, even the policing arrangements of which he told the press would see *"mounted officers outside the ground and a large number of officers under Superintendent Keys inside the ground. Those visiting Old Trafford would greatly help matters if they would make for the entrances at the far end of the enclosure, instead of flocking to the turnstiles immediately they pass over the railway bridge. Some sixty entrances will be available, and it will be as well for spectators to decide before they enter the enclosure on the place they intend to occupy, instead of afterwards transferring. The gates will be open at one o'clock."*

The Old Trafford offices were not, however, the only places where busy scenes were to witnessed. Joiners were busily engaged in preparing the telegraph office and arranging extra seats for Pressmen, while in another portion bricklayers were engaged in making an additional doorway. This was for the purpose of providing an emergency exit, which was considered to be a wise precaution in view of a tremendous crowd. Mangnall said that the reason for such alterations was *"that there will no doubt be many desirous of leaving the enclosure before the game is completed, and to have done so it would have meant opening of one the large gates, and this might have meant that those outside would have made a wild rush to gain admission to the enclosure. The new means of exit will be similar to those seen at Belle Vue."*

Mangnall had also tried to pursue a drinks licence for the ground on behalf of Alfred Wigley of the Kings Arms on Oldham Road. Strange when the dear old Dog and Partridge was just a couple of hundred yards or so up the road, but this was refused by the Manchester County Justices as they did not want supporters of the two clubs remaining overly long in the city.

With United's interest in the F.A. Cup from a competitive perspective having disappeared in east London at the end of February, the remaining eleven First Division fixtures, or however many it would take to clinch the championship, were the sole focus for players and management alike. The first fixture following the cup exit saw a 2-2 draw at Middlesbrough, followed by an emphatic 5-0 win over Preston North End and a 3-2 win over Tottenham Hotspur. Those five points kept United ahead of the pack, three clear of Aston Villa, who still had a game in hand. Third place Sunderland, who had dropped points of late, were now six points adrift giving the title race a two team look.

That picture, however, could well have changed dramatically on the afternoon of Saturday March 18th. United travelled to Notts County and lost by a solitary goal, but it was only Sunderland who made any headway in regards to catching the leaders, taking a point from their game at Bristol City. Aston Villa threw away their opportunity to close in on United by losing 1-0 at Newcastle. Seven days later, only United's name from that leading trio could be found on the list of First Division fixtures for that day, with Oldham Athletic making the relatively short journey to Old Trafford. If United had won they would have secured a five point advantage over Villa and seven over Sunderland, with only six games remaining. They would therefore be able to achieve fifty-seven points, while Villa could only amass fifty-six and Sunderland fifty-two. The record number of points by a title-winning side stood at fifty-three – obtained by Newcastle United in the 1908-09 season. Such a total was well within United's grasp. Unfortunately Oldham left Old Trafford with a point from a 0-0 draw keeping the championship bubbling away, more so as Villa took both points against Everton two days later. The destination of the trophy sat delicately balanced on a very fine thread and a slip by either club could prove fatal as the season moved into its final four weeks.

April 1st saw 'Knocker' West repay a chunk of his transfer fee with both goals in a 2-0 victory over Liverpool at Old Trafford, while Villa scraped a solitary goal victory against Middlesbrough. Sunderland drifted further out of the picture with a 1-1 draw at Tottenham. Had West not found his shooting boots, or if Liverpool had secured another Old Trafford success, then the heat would certainly have been turned up and as it was Villa remained two points behind with a game in hand.

For many, that 2-0 win over Liverpool tilted the championship in United's favour, but they were to change their minds the following Saturday. April 8th saw United travel to nearby Bury, while Villa entertained Preston North End in Birmingham and the results of that afternoon – United winning 3-0 and Villa somewhat surprisingly losing 2-0, swung the title in United's favour as they now held a four-point advantage. Villa's game in hand was now somewhat meaningless. But there was still a twist in the tale.

The hectic Easter period saw Villa beat Sheffield United 3-0 on April 14th, while twenty-four hours later, United could only draw 1-1 with the same team. That same afternoon Villa were back in action, beating Notts County 2-1, a victory that put them level on points with United, both clubs having played the same number of games. Easter Monday again saw only United in action, this time against Wednesday and once again a point was dropped, nudging the advantage Villa's way. Many were now of the opinion that those two drawn games against the Sheffield sides had cost United the championship.

Mangnall's title hopes had been dented by injuries: right-half Dick Duckworth had missed the last four fixtures while captain Charlie Roberts missed the game against Sheffield Wednesday and would go on to miss the final three games of the season. Both were influential players, two thirds of the famed 'Duckworth-Roberts-Bell' half back line that had propelled Mangnall's team to the top of the game. To compound the problems Mangnall also endured a lengthy period without the services of creator and goal-scorer George Wall. The United manager, however, was certainly not immune from criticism, as many debated his decision to move West from his preferred position of centre-forward to outside-left against Bury and the two Sheffield clubs and even though the former Forest man scored in the 1-1 draw with United. West was back as the spearhead for the penultimate fixture of the season, one that would most certainly have a huge bearing on where the First Division championship ended up, as it took Manchester United to Villa Park. Nowadays there would be days of hype on

Sky Sports about this title decider and back in Edwardian times the football press was no less hyperbolic.

As it stood, United had fifty points with two games to play, Villa had forty-eight points with three games remaining,. The Villa Park gates were closed well before kick-off on a crowd of 47,100 and the scene was set. From the kick-off Villa took the game to their opponents, forcing numerous corners before taking the lead in the fifteenth minute. Whalley fouled Wallace near the touchline and the free kick was floated into the United penalty area where Hofton appeared to mis-judge the flight of the ball, allowing Bache to run in to place the ball beyond Edmonds. It took United just five minutes to level, Halse picking up a through pass and firing home from twenty-five yards and although Anstey in the Villa goal got his fingertips to the ball, he could nothing to stop it going in just inside the post. The goal inspired United, but they failed to capitalise and were punished when Hampton scored a second for Villa ten minutes before the interval.

Meredith missed a golden opportunity early in the second half following good work between West and Halse and it was a miss he was to rue, as seventeen minutes into the second period Villa increased their advantage; Gerrish picked out Wallace who drew out the United defence before slipping the ball through to Henshall who beat Edmonds with a low shot into the far corner. Following the goal, the action was somewhat diluted, United heads went down and dropped even further when Wallace converted a penalty after Hofton fouled Hampton. At 4-1 down there was something of a glimmer of hope when Villa were reduced to ten men with fifteen minutes remaining after Hunter was sent-off for a foul on West in the Villa penalty area. But that glimmer disappeared as if by a flick of a switch, as following a conversation with his linesman, West was also ordered from the pitch for what was considered retaliation, although Halse went on to convert the resulting spot-kick. It was to prove nothing more than a consolation. Villa went to the top of the table on goal average and still had a game in hand. To all intents and purposes the title seemed done and dusted as the home fans celebrated. Still, Mangnall would no doubt have reflected that 'where there's life, there's hope' and United still had that last game to play knowing they had to win. Nevertheless the clear advantage now sat with Villa, who were also well aware as to what was required to be crowned champions, while they also had the better goal average if it should come down to that.

On April 24th Aston Villa failed to hammer home their advantage following a 0-0 draw with Blackburn Rovers. It was a result that saw them lead United by a point but it meant that everything rested on the final ninety minutes of the season as Villa travelled to Liverpool while United entertained third place Sunderland at Old Trafford. Now out of the title picture, the north-east side still had pride to play for and could cause their hosts a problem, although they had spent the previous week on a tour of Scotland and probably cared little for the forthcoming ninety minutes. Liverpool, on the other hand, languished in mid-table and looked unlikely to cause Villa many problems as the Midland side looked to hold retain the title.

At half time on the afternoon of April 29th, news filtered through to Ernest Mangnall that Liverpool were leading 2-1, having taken a two goal lead, before being pegged back. United, without Hofton, Roberts, Bell and Wall, although looking something of a miss-matched eleven, were 3-1 in front through Turnbull, West and Halse and as it stood had one hand on the championship trophy. Buoyed by the news from Merseyside United upped a gear and within ten minutes of the re-start Halse edged them closer to the title with a fourth. Turnbull added a fifth as the score across Lancashire remained the same, but by full-time, Liverpool had added a third. Villa's dream had become a nightmare and United were champions.

For Mangnall it was a noteworthy triumph, two league championships and an F. A. Cup victory in the space of four seasons had placing him on a pedestal in Mancunian football history. Only one other manager in recent football history could match his achievement − Frank Watt at Newcastle United, who had guided the Tyneside club to the league title in 1904-05, 1906-07 and 1908-09, plus the F. A. Cup in 1910. Arthur Dickinson had guided Sheffield Wednesday to the championship in 1902-03 and 1903-04, having also been an F. A. Cup winner in 1896, while Tom Watson had seen league success with Liverpool in 1900-01 and 1905-06. All, including Mangnall, had some way to go to emulate George Ramsay who guided Aston Villa to the First Division title in 1893-94; 1895-96; 1896-97; 1898-99; 1899-1900 and 1909-10, plus the F. A. Cup in 1887; 1895; 1897 and 1905.

Despite their triumphs, it is debatable if any of that quartet of excellent managers were workaholics like J. E. Mangnall. He seemed to be constantly involved in numerous projects, mainly for United, but also for the good of football in general and in June 1911 he was credited as the man behind the formation of the Central League. Writing in the 'History of the Lancashire Football Association' in 1928, Mangnall himself told the story.

> *"About half way through the month of May 1911,*
> *the League clubs had reason to complain of the*

attitude adopted by the other cubs, particularly those in the Second Division, Lancashire combination. In the past the League clubs had loyally obeyed the rules, although they had been out voted as the result of sectional meetings held for the purpose, and on one occasion an adjourned Annual Meeting was necessary. Prior to the Annual Meeting – May 1911, a caucus meeting of sixteen clubs was held. I do not pretend to a knowledge of what transpired at that meeting, but it was suggested that the club calling the meeting was anxious to have one of its members on the Management Committee; that members of the league clubs should be opposed, particularly those from Bolton. However that may be, it is significant that Messrs. J. J. Bentley, T. Y. Ritson and J. T. Howcroft were thrown off the Committee.

"The League clubs were indignant and determined not to tolerate these caucus meetings any longer. As Secretary of the Club, I knew that Manchester United had not only made up its mind to withdraw from the Lancashire Combination, but that its intention was to make an application for admission to one of the Manchester Leagues. I then submitted a scheme to Mr. J. H. Davies, President and he gave me authority to proceed carte blanche as best I thought. Of the clubs interviewed I got promises of support from Bolton Wanderers, Bury, Crewe Alexandra, Glossop, Manchester City, Manchester United, Oldham Athletic, Preston North End, Stockport County and Southport Central.

"An idea at the time – if no more clubs linked

up – was to fill the vacant Saturdays by means of a subsidiary competition. After an Annual General Meeting of the L.F.A. at the Winter Gardens, Blackpool, on May 24th 1911, I called a private meeting. The following clubs were represented; Blackpool, Blackburn Rovers, Bolton Wanderers, Burnley, Bury, Everton, Liverpool, Manchester City, Manchester United, Oldham Athletic and Preston North End. Mr. W. A. Wilkinson (Manchester City), was invited to take the Chair, Mr. W. C. Cuff (Everton) was requested to act as Honorary Secretary, pro. tem."

"The members present strongly condemned the recent actions of the non-League clubs, and expressed their willingness to withdraw from Membership of the Lancashire Combination, although several were unable to pledge their clubs until they had discussed and considered the position. It was resolved that the League clubs, Members of the Lancashire Combination, resign from the Combination, and form a new League, and that application be made to the F. A. for affiliation, and that a meeting of the members be held in Manchester on a date to be fixed by a Sub-Committee to consider name, rules etc.

"At a meeting of the Sub-Committee, held in the Imperial Hotel, on London Road, on May 29th 1911, it was resolved: 'That the new League be called the Central League. It was unanimously resolved that the League consist of eighteen clubs.'"

During the Summer of 1911 much of Mangnall's pre-season work had been taken up helping to prepare a prospectus for the flotation of the club which would be forwarded to the authorities for their approval. United had no intention of falling foul of the game's administrators again. He had not been as busy as some might have expected during the summer months, while he had reduced his playing staff to twenty-six. Critical voices had also been heard in relation to the price of season tickets for the stand, as it was felt that two guineas was too much to ask and by setting that price, sales would be down. How much of a say Mangnall had in such matters can only be debated.

The 1911-12 season got underway with a 0-0 draw at Hyde Road against Manchester City, but two defeats, a further two draws and four wins, over the course of those opening two months left United in a comfortable sixth place, two points behind leaders Middlesbrough. Mangnall also clinched yet another trophy with an incredible 8-4 win in the FA Charity Shield at Stamford Bridge over Southern League champions Swindon Town.

Mangnall's work on the club's flotation proved successful as the Football Association officials, following an "exhaustive enquiry" were satisfied with everything that the club had put in place and that it was now working "on a satisfactory basis".

November saw defeats to Tottenham, at home, and Liverpool away, coupled with a goalless draw at home to Preston North End, the only success coming against Aston Villa at Old Trafford. Being six points behind leaders Newcastle United was far from ideal, but it was a picture that was to alter only slightly by the end of the year, despite four victories and two draws from seven fixtures played.

Five points behind the league leaders and with a game

in hand at the halfway stage of the season was a position many would have accepted, particularly neighbours City, who found themselves occupying a far from creditable third from bottom spot. However, if Mangnall had eyes set on a third First Division title then they disappeared during a disastrous January. A 2-0 win over Woolwich Arsenal at Old Trafford, that saw United bounce up into third place and were boosted by the fact that leaders Newcastle United were beaten 2-1 at Sheffield United. The gap at the top was a mere three points and there was still that game in hand but from the other five league fixtures across January and February 1912 United claimed just one solitary point from a 0-0 draw against Bury at Old Trafford. Not only that, they were to score only one goal, in a 2-1 home defeat by West Bromwich Albion on January 20th. Trips to Everton, Sunderland and Sheffield Wednesday resulted in 4-0, 5-0 and 3-0 defeats respectively. United, who had been dubbed 'the best team in the world' only a year earlier, now languished in tenth, nine points adrift of the leaders.

The season had taken on a look similar to that of 1908-09 when the end of March, beginning of April had witnessed a run of four games without a win or a goal, or if you stretched the current campaign back to just after that win over Arsenal on January 1st and up to April 17th it was a horrendous time with only one win, four draws [two of those goal less] and nine defeats. The heavy defeats hinted at something more than poor form and it was far and away Mangnall's worst spell in the league whilst at the club.

That 1908-09 season had brought success in the F. A. Cup and for a while it looked as though history might repeat itself in 1912. Round one saw Huddersfield Town dismissed 3-1, while round two saw Coventry City suffer a similar fate, beaten 5-1 on their home turf. The third round, however, brought a slightly tougher task, as a replay was required to dispose of Reading, who held United to a 1-1 draw before being dumped out of the competition at Old Trafford on the back of a 3-0 defeat. A Walmsley own goal in the fourth round tie against Blackburn Rovers, First Division leaders at the time, earned a replay from an exciting encounter but it took an additional half hour at Ewood Park to deny Mangnall a semi-final place. United had, at one point, held a 2-0 advantage, but the home side hit back, scoring four – United's season was over, although the dismal league run ended in the third last game of the season with a 3-1 win over Oldham Athletic. This was followed by a 1-1 draw at Bolton, with the curtain coming down with a 3-1 success over champions Blackburn Rovers at Old Trafford.

It was a fitting finale.

10: The Chameleon

ENVIOUS GLANCES HAD BEEN cast over the smokey roof tops and across the cobbled streets between Hyde Road and Old Trafford in recent times. Although founded a mere two years apart, Manchester City had, like United, begun life in a completely different guise - St Mark's (West Gorton) in 1880, before morphing into Ardwick two years later. April 1894 saw them once again go through a transformation taking up the name Manchester City. In the intervening years they had slipped behind their red shirted neighbours in the footballing stakes. An F. A. Cup success in 1903-04 and Second Division titles in 1898-99, 1902-03 and 1909-10 were their only honours. Neither could they boast of a home anywhere near as lavish as Old Trafford.

The reason behind the lack of silverware over Hyde Road way, in recent years at least, was down to one man, okay two if you want to once again throw in the financial clout of J. H. Davies, but without J. E. Mangnall in charge who knows what Manchester United's list of honours would show. Mangnall had snatched City's erring individuals from their grasp, had brought the F. A. Cup and the First Division championship to United, whilst seeing the club's bank account boosted through the additional revenue that the move to Old Trafford had brought. However, despite such success, all was not well down by the Ship Canal as hinted at by the disastrous form of the previous season where the team had been winless for months having been in a position to challenge for the title. Something was afoot…

If Ernest Mangnall was unhappy, he had kept it to himself, or at least within the four walls of his home. He had taken the club to untold heights and achieved the impossible considering they had almost gone out of business a decade earlier but now stood at the top of the English game, a by word for success and a name known throughout the land and the world – Manchester United.

Not that it had all been plain-sailing, there had been bitter pills to swallow, most notable among them was Old Trafford not being built to his initial plans, there being no concrete running track for instance. Another, more pressing concern, was that unlike at the start of his reign there was no money available to strengthen the team, which was now showing some signs of wear and tear. The latter problem was no doubt caused by the ongoing investigations of the F.A. who had always resented the naked ambition of both Manchester clubs but these were matters that did not sit well with Mr Mangnall. There was also a third point that may well have played a telling factor in his cross-town move – money. Not a chequebook with which to sign talented individuals, so much as his personal remuneration.

Pre-season training for the 1912-13 campaign got underway at the beginning of August and the only new face to be seen within the United ranks was Beale, a goalkeeper who had been signed from Norwich City. Manchester City on the other hand had made an audacious £1500 bid for United's centre-half and captain Charlie Roberts. Somewhat strangely Roberts expressed a "strong desire" to move to Hyde Road. Blackburn Rovers had also tried to lure Enoch West away from Old Trafford, offering United £1200 for their centre-forward.

Despite that cheeky bid for Roberts, City had been otherwise idle in the transfer market but there had been activity behind closed doors. August 1st had seen the contract of City secretary Mr. J. H. Newbould expire. The former Derby County man had taken up the post six years previously and had no knowledge that his contract would not be renewed. A letter in the *Athletic News* spoke of Newbould as being "as straight as an arrow" and that his personal conduct, his industry and his knowledge of the game and players was first class. The writer also described the action of the City board as being "cruel", adding: "*The fact of the matter is, I suppose, that Manchester City decided to have a change; to see if a new secretary would bring new fortune.*"

'Tityrus', one of the main writers in the *Athletic News* was equally critical of the board's methods, writing in the paper's edition of Monday August 5th:

> "*On Tuesday evening Mr. H. J. Newbould was the secretary of Manchester City. On Wednesday morning Mr. Newbould was no longer in office. I fail to see much breadth of view, generosity of feeling, or even sense of justice in the manner in which the directors of the City have behaved to their principal official. Let us look at this unpleasant subject little closely. When Manchester City were convicted by the Football Association of serious offences against the regulation of clubs, and deprived of their players who had received large sums of money to which they were not entitled, Mr. Newbould went from Derby County to Manchester City. His record at Derby must have satisfied the board, or he would never have been engaged. He was given an agreement, and that agreement was renewed -*

without pressure. For six years Mr. Newbould has been the secretary. Now his second agreement was due to expire on August. 1, Thursday last, when the players came up for training. Last Tuesday evening the agenda paper for the board contained the item: Consideration of the renewal of the secretary's agreement. Mr. Newbould retired, and the subject was debated for an hour and the matter adjourned until the following morning. On Wednesday Mr. Newbould was called into the room and told that the board had decided not to renew his agreement. He was given the option of resigning but refused to do so. Naturally he inquired the reason why he was thus instantly dismissed. None was given. Apparently, none will be given."

City had finished sixth from bottom in the 1911-12 season, just two points above relegated Preston North End, but only two adrift of United in thirteenth. What transpired prior to that board meeting and in the two weeks or so after it, no one knows exactly, but much can be read between the lines, as on the evening of Tuesday August 20th, Ernest Mangnall was appointed the new secretary/manager of Manchester City. It didn't come as much of a surprise to those in the know, as some of the newspapers that morning had suggested that such an appointment was a possibility. The *Dundee Courier* – *"It is just possible that the United will lose the help of Mr E. Mangnall, the secretary and manager of the club. It is well known that Manchester City are in search of such an official, and it is understood that Mr Mangnall has been offered the post."*

So, the man who had done so much for Manchester United had gone. There is nothing to say that the United directors made any attempt to try and persuade him to stay, nor does there seem to be any lengthy consideration on Mangnall's part as regards making the change from red to blue. Of his departure Billy Meredith was to say:

> *"The Manchester United team will, of course, greatly miss Ernest Mangnall, who has left to manage Manchester City. Even though he and the Directors of Manchester United have not agreed on a number of matters, there is no doubt that Ernest Mangnall was a very fine manager. No man in the country, except perhaps Will Cuff of Everton, could have run such a club with so much success on so low a cost. I should say that Mr. Mangnall and Mr. Cuff stand alone in the management world. Mr Mangnall is about the best judge of a player serving a club in England. Apart from that, the new Manchester City manager knows how to buy and sell at the best profit to his own club. He should do well at Hyde Road. If he succeeds, he will probably make enemies, because it is well known that he is to have a free hand. I know him, and I feel confident that he will not be content until the club is run at a big profit."*

City's season kicked off on Monday September 2nd at Notts County with a favourable 1-0 victory, but there is some debate as to when Ernest's Hyde Road career actually began. Some say that on that Monday afternoon he should have been in London where United faced Woolwich Arsenal, but instead he could be found in Nottingham watching his new batch of players. The following Saturday it becomes equally confusing as by a strange quirk of fate, the fixture list paired United with

City at Old Trafford, ninety minutes that was set aside as being a 'benefit' match for Billy Meredith. It is therefore perhaps best to leave the matter in the hands of the national press of that time. The *Star Green 'Un*:

> *"That was quite a unique position in which Mr. Mangnall occupied on Saturday. He was the City secretary-elect, but had not finished his engagement with United, so in reality, he had what could be considered as control of both teams."* The Scottish Referee *in its brief summary of the game contained the following:* "Meredith's Benefit - The 'Battle of Manchester' between Manchester United and Manchester City attracted an attendance of over 40,000 spectators, the gate receipts totalling over £1,400. With tickets sold and subscriptions, it is expected that the popular Welshman will gather £2,000, an easy record for a footballer. Manchester City won somewhat luckily by a goal scored per Wynn. Mr J. E. Mangnall, the United manager, takes up his new duties with the 'Citizens' on Monday, and to him the win was especially gratifying. It was, as usual, a keenly-contested match, no quarter being asked or given by either side. Meredith captained the United team for the day, and was the subject of a magnificent ovation."*

No matter where his favours lay that afternoon, there appeared to be no hard feelings from the United Board as following the match against City, Mr. J. H. Davies presented the out-going secretary with a silver table ornament and his wife with a gold wristwatch on behalf of the United board, wishing him well in his new post.

Before progressing to Hyde Road, it is perhaps

worth making the observation that following Mangnall's departure from Old Trafford United went downhill. With assistant secretary T. J. Wallworth at the helm for just over a month before J. J. Bentley took over, what was effectively Mangnall's team finished a creditable fourth at the end of the 1912-13 season, but then the club hit a downward spiral, free-fall even, which saw Manchester United plummet to the Second Division within five seasons. In the seasons that followed Mangnall's departure, which saw further changes in manager with the appointment of J. R. Robson in 1914, until 1921, and J. A. Chapman from 1921 until 1926, United finished 14th, 18th, 12th, 13th and then in 1921-22, 22nd. It was therefore Second Division fare at Old Trafford for the following three seasons. Did Ernest jump ship just before the inevitable crash or was the crash due to him jumping ship?

Mangnall settled quickly into his new cross-town post and had it not been for two defeats in mid-October then City would have found themselves at the top of the First Division. 'Content' would perhaps be a better word than 'happy' to use for the new manager's first few weeks in charge, as despite holding fifth spot, three points behind leaders Aston Villa with two games in hand, City had scored twenty goals fewer, although on the plus side, they had conceded six less. Goals were never something that Mangnall's United side had ever been short of as all the front line were more than capable of finding the net on a regular basis, with the half-back line always happy to step forward when required. At Hyde Road, however, if Wallace, Jones, Howard or Wynn didn't manage to score, then more often than not, no-one did. Throughout that 1912-13 league campaign City failed to score on ten occasions yet despite this Mangnall still failed to sign a goal scoring forward.

Although there was no glut of goals, the action at Hyde Road still managed to pull in the crowds which averaged out at around 20,000, although around 10,000 more could often be found there if the opposition was more to their taste. The visit of United on December 28th, when City failed to score in a 2-0 defeat, pulled in just over 36,000, but this was overshadowed a couple of months later when 41,709 gained admission for the second round F. A. Cup tie with Sunderland. Mangnall had found himself inundated with requests for tickets and would have been well aware that a large crowd was expected. At 2.07pm the Hyde Road gates were locked with too many inside and thousands still outside. Those outside were soon inside, as gates were broken down. Half an hour before kick-off many were swarming over the pitch and although quickly reinforced, the local constabulary were still unable to cope with the vast crowd. As the referee and linesmen strode onto the pitch they were quickly surrounded by the crowd, but eventually the officials were able to get the match underway, after the touch-line and goal-lines were re-marked. The crowd were forced back as far as they could go.

The game kicked-off nineteen minutes late and between the players taking the field and the half-time whistle, one hour and twenty minutes had elapsed. The interval lasted sixteen minutes and before play could resume the lines had once again to be re-marked due to the vast numbers that had trodden across the turf. The groundsman's efforts were, however, to no avail, as the second half was to last a mere fifteen minutes, before the referee called time as the fading light made it impossible to finish the game.

In the aftermath Sunderland pointed the finger directly at the City management citing gross negligence, while even the local *Daily Citizen* newspaper reported that although City asserted that they were victims of the circumstances, *"This is surely a confession of weakness, for if they were taken by surprise the City club lulled itself into a false state of security which no one else of experience did. For weeks it was drummed into them that they had the great event of the round, and save for the Oldham Athletic match, they were without rivals for a considerable area around Manchester."*

Three days after the abandoned tie the Football Association Council met in London and following the draw for the third round and the appointing of the relevant match officials, City were hauled onto the carpet. Sunderland claimed the match as they were leading 2-0 at the time, while City were of the opinion that "the conditions were exceptional and unparalleled" and asked for the match to be replayed. Reports from the match officials accompanied letters from both clubs, while Mangnall and Wilkinson were present as representatives of City.

Much to Sunderland's annoyance, the game was ordered to be replayed, but at least they took something from the fact that it was to be replayed at Roker Park with a possible replay scheduled for Bramall Lane, Sheffield. City were left red-faced and fined £500, £350 of that going to local charities and the balance to the F. A. Benevolent Fund. City paid an even bigger price as they lost the re-arranged tie 2-0. The replay itself wasn't completed without its own problems as once again the gates were locked, despite admission prices being doubled and the ground far from full, which resulted in many intent upon seeing the game scurrying away to find a suitable vantage point from which to view as much of the game as possible. Some fifty men and youths clambered up onto the roof of a coal depot close to the ground only for it to collapse, the majority falling thirty feet to the ground.

The threat posed by huge crowds was to remain a thorn in Mangnall's side as the season progressed; the visit of Sheffield Wednesday on April 12th was seen as being under threat after a postcard was sent to him, apparently by members of the Suffragette movement, something that was gathering momentum and causing untold problems across the country, which read: *"No match on Saturday unless Mrs. Pankhurst is released. Votes For Women."* City failed to release an official statement at the time, but were relieved that the game proceeded without any problems.

Mangnall's first season in charge at Hyde Road stuttered to an end with only one win in the final five games. They finished sixth, two places behind United, although many were of the opinion that the position of superiority in Manchester would change in the months and years ahead.

The following season looked as though it would be much of the same for City. 'Pilgrim' in the *Athletic News* writing prior to the commencement of that 1913–14 season:

> *"Whilst, from the support they are accorded, few clubs can better afford to follow the fashion in the way of heavy transfer fees, probably none have expended less in this direction than Manchester City. They have resolutely set their backs against such extravagance, the policy of Mr. J. E. Mangnall and his directors being to find the players they want in as near a literal sense as possible, and so it is*

that, as far as reputation goes, the ranks of the club will not be illuminated by any brilliant stars.

"To a considerable extent the City will rely upon the players who wore the colours of the club last season, all of whom, with the exception of Jobling, Kelly, and Lawrence, are available. There are not likely to be any great changes to begin with, at any rate. Their chief defect last winter was the absence of capable reserves. This was reflected in the comparative failure of the Central League team, and it is in this direction that Mr. Mangnall has mainly devoted his attention. He has enlisted the services of ten new men, each and all of whom has still his reputation to make in first-class football, but the City secretary is noted for a seeing eye, and on the form the men have shown in the trial games his judgment would not appear to have been very far wrong. Forwards were the chief necessity, and it is significant that seven of the newcomers are for this department."

Across town, where J. J. Bentley was now in charge, it was worth noting that the half-back line of Duckworth, Roberts and Bell had been broken up with Roberts going to Oldham Athletic and Bell to Blackburn Rovers. United were showing the first signs of a slide that wouldn't be arrested until the arrival of Matt Busby.

If Mangnall's first season in charge at Hyde Road was considered favourable, then his second could be classed as unsatisfactory, with goalscoring once again proving to be something of a problem with thirteen of the thirty-eight fixtures producing only one in the goals for column and a further ten being blank. Only one of the opening twelve games was to end in victory, although it was felt that by the turn of the year they had "found speed, combination and skill."

Sitting in his Hyde Road office in February 1914, Mangnall had much to contemplate. City had been drawn at home to Sheffield United in the fourth round of the F. A. Cup and he was well aware that he could not risk the catastrophe of the previous season. Hyde Road was considered by the *Sheffield Green 'Un* as being *"too antiquated for the complete setting of modern Cup-tie spectacles. The stand accommodation is poor, while all told, the ground will not hold more than 40,000."*

He contemplated long and hard about going cap in hand to United and asking to borrow Old Trafford for the afternoon, whilst considering Sheffield United's suggestion of having the minimum admission price fixed at one shilling, as they believed that at ordinary prices, far too many people would assemble. In the end Sheffield United officials refused to agree to boys being admitted at half price and there was no admittance below sixpence while a shift to Old Trafford was out of the question.

Thankfully for Mangnall and City, the Sheffield United cup-tie passed without incident. Had there been any crowd problems then the weight of the Football Association would have fallen on their shoulders. The tie actually took three games to decide with the Yorkshire side winning 1-0 at Villa Park. On the First Division front the season drew to a close somewhat favourably, with only one defeat in the final half dozen games, but thirteenth was hardly a position that anyone connected with City looked favourably upon. It would have been fourteenth, but they had a better goal difference than neighbours United.

As he had at United, Mangnall looked into taking his

Manchester City side on an end of season continental trip, but this time around there would be no games involved. It was simply seen as a 'thank you', a trip for the players to relax away from the rigours of football and life in Manchester. Mangnall therefore contacted the Football League Management Committee asking their permission to pay his players 'out of pocket expenses' and as to how much they were permitted to pay. Permission was refused, as it was "contrary to the rules" and therefore could not be allowed. Disappointed, Mangnall took himself off to Scotland.

Mangnall's arrival at Manchester United had not produced instant success and it was proving likewise at Hyde Road, but unlike his time with his former employers there was no bottomless purse. He did, however, have a shrewd eye for a promising player and had brought the likes of Tommy Browell, the club's leading goal scorer in 1913-14, from Everton for £1,450 in October 1913. If the City directorate preferred to keep a tight hold of the purse strings, then Mangnall had the persuasive methods which enabled him now and again to prise them apart and therefore allow himself the opportunity to dabble in the transfer market. No sooner had the curtains closed on the 1913-14 season than he had managed to secure the club chequebook and pen a figure of £2,000 for the signature of Horace Barnes from Derby County. This was a considerable sum but such was the need for a goalscorer at Hyde Road that Mangnall had no hesitation in splashing the cash. Derby had been just been relegated, gates had dropped and cash was required, but there were no giveaways, as clubs were informed that the likes of Barnes would not be leaving for anything less than £2,000. Strangely United had also been interested in the player, but when they were told the price, they walked away. Of the transfer Mangnall said, *"his task in signing the player had been one of the most difficult with which he had ever been faced."* He had been helped by the fact that Barnes was engaged to be married to a Manchester lady, and wanted to join one of the Manchester clubs, but with seven of the score or so of clubs who were interested and prepared to exceed £2,000 it was no mean feat to forestall the opposition. When asked if he would care to state the exact amount he had paid, Mangnall said he would not, but, he added, *"you can say it exceeds £2,000"*, adding: *"it is against our policy to pay such sums for players, but we recognised that such loyalty as the supporters displayed was worthy of only the highest class of football, and they were doing their best to provide it."* He was now of the opinion that in Barnes, Browell and Taylor, City had three of the finest inside forwards in the country.

If the City directors were reluctant or concerned about allowing Mangnall to splash out £2,000 on Barnes, it was perhaps due to the fact that they had more expensive plans in place – moving to a new ground. Hyde Road had become inadequate for City's needs, it could boast of having cover on all four sides, something that Old Trafford couldn't, but there was considerable difficulty in making any expansion to accommodate more supporters due to its proximity to the railway and Galloway's Boiler Works, although a Manchester estate agent had been negotiating with the Great Central Railway Company over an increased holding capacity, which would have seen the ground turned round and various extensions made at a cost of around £20,000.

At the club AGM in May 1914 it was announced that they had failed to come to terms with the railway company and instead had obtained an option on what they considered as being a suitable site for a new ground at Belle Vue, Gorton. The club accounts showed City to be in good health, with gates standing at something of a record, particularly in the Central League. However within weeks all thoughts about moving to a new ground and the summer holiday on the continent were suddenly far from the minds of the City management, players and supporters, as the world was plunged into turmoil following the assassination of the Austro-Hungarian heir, Archduke Ferdinand, in Sarajevo on June 28th, an event that triggered the Great War.

Initially it was presumed that the conflict in Europe would be short-lived, so the 1914–15 season kicked off as normal, Mangnall had made one or two further alterations to his squad and had a positive outlook as regards the season ahead, but was given something of a shock when khaki clad officers of the 15th Battalion of the Manchester Artillery knocked on his office door to inform him that Hyde Road was being commandeered by the authorities in order to stable some three hundred horses, something that led to considerable damage to the pitch.

1914–15 was a strange season for all concerned. Even before the first ball was kicked the Football League and the Football Association had been in contact with all clubs informing them that in conjunction with their regular football training, players had to undergo drill and rifle instruction. Mangnall consulted with the local military authorities in regards to bringing the necessary instructors to Hyde Road. As a follow-up to these directives, he put pen to paper following a board meeting of the City directorate on Wednesday September 23rd, writing to the other local clubs – Manchester United, Bolton Wanderers,

Blackburn Rovers, Bury, Stockport County, Oldham Athletic, Stalybridge Celtic, Liverpool, Everton, Preston North End, and Burnley:

> *"It has occurred to my directors that the question of co-operative military training and shooting, subject to proper supervision, should be taken up by the whole of the League clubs in Lancashire. My directors think that this question has probably already appealed to all the clubs, but as to the question of convening a meeting it may be that what is everybody's business has been nobody's business. With this apology, my directors ask you, either by one or more representatives of your club, to meet them at the Pack Horse Hotel, Bolton, on Thursday, October 1, at 3 p.m.— Yours faithfully, J. E. MANGNALL."*

At that meeting, at which only Liverpool and Everton were missing as they were already in the process of erecting rifle ranges for their players, a sub-committee was formed in order to carry out the scheme and the clubs present were recommended to go in for drilling, with a proposal of a joint drill on a monthly basis.

At the end of the opening month of the new season City found themselves in the unfamiliar position of heading the First Division, undefeated in their opening five fixtures. They were still there as November arrived and still unbeaten, although as per normal their 'goals for' column was considerably less than that of the three clubs below them. By the end of the year they had surrendered pole position to Oldham Athletic, having lost three games in the interim. Their 'goals for' showed twenty-two fewer than the league leaders and fourteen fewer than third placed Everton. Oh how Mangnall yearned for a Turnbull, Halse, Bannister or Wall, as his recent acquisition, Barnes, had only scored thrice.

As the weeks and months passed and the conflict in Europe continued without any sign of abating, Mangnall became heavily involved in the 'War Effort'. With Christmas on the horizon he found some of his time taken up with making the necessary arrangements for the dispatch of 4,500 boxes of cigarettes, each with a personal message from the Manchester City board, to every soldier serving in the 4th Battalion of the Manchester Regiment at the front line.

As things became more serious, more and more footballers enlisted. Mid-December saw forty London-based players join the Footballers' Battalion – the 17th (Service) Battalion of the Middlesex Regiment. When asked by a reporter of the *Manchester Courier* if he knew of any such enlisting of Lancashire-based players, Mangnall replied: "Not as yet", adding that the London clubs were nearer to each other than their Lancashire counterparts and the distance that they had to travel to a training centre would be much closer than the local players. He went on to add: *"This was the point that knocked on the head the scheme put forward by Manchester City for forming a volunteer battalion of players of the first-class Lancashire clubs."* Mangnall also wrote cheques to the Manchester Royal Infirmary Board – £10. 10s, towards the treatment of military patients and £50 to a fund set up on behalf of wounded Belgian soldiers.

Having fallen from the heady height of leadership of the First Division, City never returned. Having begun 1915 with league and cup victories, things quickly deteriorated, Chelsea progressed into the fourth round of the F. A. Cup on the back of a 1-0 victory at Hyde Road, while the remaining three months of the season fizzled out like a damp squib, with only three victories in the last fifteen games of the season with seven defeats, six of which saw City's much attack draw blanks, they still managed to finish a respectable fifth.

Respectable was not a word used across Manchester following events at Old Trafford 2nd April 1915. United, languishing third from bottom of the First Division, played host to thirteenth-placed Liverpool and recorded a surprise 2-0 victory, but handbills were soon distributed around the city claiming that the game was fixed and the match was soon subject to an FA enquiry which ended in December 1915 concluding, *"we are satisfied that a number of them* [players] *were party to an arrangement to join together to obtain money by betting on the actual result of the match. We are satisfied that the allegations have been proved against the following – Liverpool – J. Sheldon, R. R. Purcell, T. Hiller, C. T. Fairfoull. Manchester United – A. Turnbull, A. Whalley, E. J. West and L. Cook of Chester. They are all permanently suspended from taking any part in football or football management, and shall not be allowed to enter any football ground in the future."* The Football Association went on to add that it was of the opinion that others were also involved *"but as the penalty is severe, we have restricted our findings to those as to whose offence there is no reasonable doubt."*

How Cook was involved is anyone's guess and was something that was never proved, but one other player found himself in hot water – Fred Howard of Manchester City, who was suspended for twelve months due to *"the contradictory manner in which he gave evidence before the committee."* Who knows what Mangnall thought about it all, as he knew the United players involved well, and more so in regards to Howard's involvement, leaving him to ponder the idea of there being other City players involved who had escaped undetected.

What was behind that match fixing episode? Was it the fact that United were dicing with relegation, or was it simply a case of the players looking to supplement their weekly wages? None were to ever reveal the true story, although Enoch West was to claim his innocence for the next thirty years and never played football again. Sandy Turnbull was another who never kicked a ball again, as he was killed in action at Arras on May 3rd 1917.

At the AGM of the Football League in the Connaught Rooms in London in July 1915, it was decided to suspend the normal League competitions for the 1915-16 season, but a number of competitions would be arranged as far as possible, but if any club wished to not participate then that was fine. Players would also be entitled to play for any club, except outwith England, without actually being transferred.

Season 1915-16 saw City and all their near neighbours play in what was called the War League Lancashire Section and also the Southern Division of the Lancashire Section. The first taking place between September and February, the second between March and April, and at long last Ernest Mangnall could walk around Hyde Road and indeed all of Manchester with a wide smile across his face. In the past it had been goals that had deprived City of a place amongst the honours, but now, in what was an 'unofficial' season, they couldn't stop scoring. It had been something of a rare occasion for them to notch up more than two goals a game but during that first half of the 1915-16 season Mangnall rejoiced in score lines such as 5-4 against Bury, 5-0 against Southport Central and 8-0 against Preston North End, all at Hyde Road. The majority of those goals came from Barnes who was justifying his large fee at last and Peter Fairclough, who had arrived with his brother Arthur, along with James Abbott from Eccles Borough in the summer of 1913, having scored seventy-one goals between them in the Lancashire Combination during the 1912-13 season. Such a wealth of goals and positive results saw City win that Lancashire Section, two points ahead of Burnley and in the second Southern Division Section, they again came out on top on 'goal ratio' ahead of Everton. Who would have thought such a thing was possible?

It is worth noting that Mangnall had also conducted a shrewd piece of business that went a considerable way to the success in that second tournament when he procured the services of Billy Meredith for the latter half of the season, the Welshman joining his old boss in a player/coach capacity. Throughout the war, Mangnall continued to be heavily involved in all aspects of the game and kept City's name at the forefront of numerous off the field matters, helping those less fortunate than himself, something he was able to do with the backing of the City board. It was reported in June 1916 that in addition to giving free admission to over 25,000 soldiers during the course of the past season, they had provided the wounded with cigarettes at every match, whilst contributing £1,125 to various charitable organisations.

Football was to take on a similar format for the next three seasons as the Great War continued across Europe. The game should perhaps have come to a halt during this time, but it was felt that the people who remained at home were in need of some recreational activity. With many men called into the forces crowds dropped dramatically, with City averaging anywhere between 3,000 and 15,000.

Mangnall's predicament in fielding a team became more of a concern by the end of the 1916-17 season when some twenty-six of his players were reported as being in the services. By the end of August it had increased to thirty with one, Paddy McGuire, reported as being lost in action, while Mangnall's big money signing – Horace Barnes had written to his manager, wishing him a successful season, whilst adding as something of a postscript that he had received a shrapnel wound to the wrist when a shell had burst, killing thirteen and wounding nine of his comrades as they were entering the trenches.

Letters to Mangnall from his players who were involved in the war slipped through the Hyde Road letter box with regularity. One came from Sidney Hoad who wrote that in a recent match behind the lines he had scored six goals, which he added was something of a change for him. Another came from Fred Howard who told of how the boat he was on had been torpedoed when only an hour out of port. Such messages must have left Mangnall wondering how many of his players would return to Hyde Road at war's end.

In previous seasons the City manager had been able to rely mainly on his own players, but for the 1917-18 campaign it was more than likely that the majority of those who appeared in a light blue shirt would be unfamiliar 'guests', although he had managed to add three young players to his depleted ranks.

Continuing his avid, sometimes fanatical, pursuit in helping those caught up in the atrocities of the war, Mangnall addressed the following letter to the secretary of the Football League in November 1917:

"My dear Charnley, Seeing Mr. M'Kenna and

Mr. Sutcliffe in Manchester on Saturday, I took the opportunity of suggesting to them that matches ought to be played for the benefit of players maimed in this terrible war, dependents of those players losing their lives, and others serving their country in many various ways, such as munitions, etc.

"Since the war commenced charity matches have been the means of raising thousands of pounds for many very deserving charitable objects, but as yet nothing has been done to create a National Fund for clubs' players serving their country in many various ways and players who are assisting us to carry on.

"If the League - and am sure they are sufficiently sympathetic - would arrange for these charity matches to take place the first Saturday in May in each year, and, if needs be, the second Saturday as well, the fund would soon reach dimensions that it would be a really lasting credit to all those who associated themselves with such a noble cause.

"As you are no doubt aware, Corporations, firms, and employers in plenty are putting aside for their employees who are serving their country a big percentage, and, in some cases, the full amount of wages their men were getting before joining up.

"The players in the Army are receiving Army pay only, and at present there is no fund from which they may receive assistance. I suggest matches on international lines on the first Saturday in May in each year, and, as previously mentioned, if need be, the second Saturday as well, one in London, one in the Midlands, and one in Lancashire until

we have obtained the many thousands of pounds which ought to accrue.

"Trusting the matter will receive early and favourable consideration. —Yours sincerely J. E. Mangnall."

In response to the above letter, the Football Association decided to hand over a sum of £5,000 to a National War Fund and they acknowledged their indebtedness to Mangnall for his initial involvement.

Season 1918-19 saw Mangnall once again guide City to first place in the Lancashire Section Subsidiary Tournament, nudging out Stoke City on 'goal ratio', while notching up a few favourable scores in the initial principal Tournament, such as 7-0 against Bury along with 6-1 and 5-1 victories over Port Vale on successive Saturdays. Horace Barnes was once again the fans' favourite with sixteen goals in eighteen appearances and they were eager to see him back in truly competitive action when normal League fixtures resumed the following season.

It was back to some form of normality for the 1919-1920 season following the armistice yet British life would never be quite the same for some considerable time with few families escaping the horrors of the 4 year conflict.

Despite everything, City could still announce a profit for the 1918-19 season and Mangnall told a packed AGM in May 1919 that he had twenty players already secured for the following season. He also told the assembled shareholders that some 59,267 soldiers had been admitted free to home games during the past season and that a sum of over £600 had been raised for charities and since the war had commenced, he was proud to say that the club had raised £3,100 for needy concerns.

Mangnall's controversial move to Manchester City didn't bring any trophies but his war work ensured his reputation grew in the city.

Mangnall's final contribution to Mancunian football was the opening of Maine Road in 1923, a stadium that City would call home for the next 80 years.

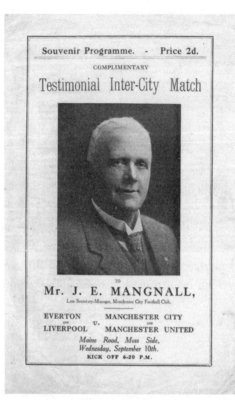

Such was the esteem in which Mr Mangnall was held that a testimonial was held in his honour between a combined Manchester team and a combined Merseyside XI.

With London, Midlands and North-East clubs back in the fold, City found things a little tougher. Barnes and Browell were back among the goals, sharing forty-five, but Mangnall had to be content with a seventh place finish. He also had to be content at being unable to select Billy Meredith, as the aging outside-right had to return to United. Having played over one hundred war-time games for City, Meredith was keen to remain at Hyde Road, but when he asked United for a free transfer they refused, meaning that any interested club would have to pay a transfer fee for the Welshman.

Meredith somewhat reluctantly returned to United and played a further thirty-five games in a red shirt, before finally re-joining City in July 1921, claiming the unique distinction of being the only individual to have played League fixtures at Hyde Road, Bank Street, Old Trafford and Maine Road.

The war had done little to help Mangnall's quest in emulating his achievements with Manchester United. Who is to say that had it not been for the conflict he would not have taken City to the League title or the F.A. Cup? Results in the regional league had been satisfactory and kicking off post-war football with seventh place, stepping up to second at the end of 1920-21 indicated that he still had that influence and capability of achieving things, but he was now getting on in years and had much more on his plate than picking a team and answering whatever correspondence came his way.

One letter of interest landed on Mangnall's desk in mid-October 1920 addressed to his chairman Mr L. F. Furness, from his old colleague at Old Trafford Mr J. H. Davies. It read: *"I have been greatly impressed by the statements in the daily papers as to the danger caused by overcrowding at your home matches, the numbers that you have had to turn away, and the great risks which are run by the football-loving public when attending a match on the City ground. I have consulted my co-directors, and am now able to offer, in the name of Manchester United, the use of our ground for your home matches until such time as you are able to offer suitable accommodation on your own ground.*

"No doubt your co-directors, when consulted, will express their views as to the way in which the suggestion should be carried out, and a formal agreement entered into with the approbation of the English League Management Committee, and I shall be pleased to hear that you and your co-directors are willing to accept the offer in the spirit in which it is made, thus cementing the amicable relations which ought always to obtain between the two premier clubs."

City's home gates for the opening games of that 1920–21 season had seen something of a post-war boom ranging between 30,000 and 40,000 on a regular basis, but they could not match the 66,000 that witnessed the first 'derby' match of the season at Old Trafford in November. The Hyde Road gates had to be closed prior to kick-off for the first home fixture of the season against Aston Villa with 35,000 inside, while the national press wrote following the fixture against Bolton Wanderers the following month that *"Hyde Road would not hold all the thousands who wished to see the match, but forty thousand got in"* and the *Sheffield Daily Telegraph* added: *"The Manchester City directors must have sighed for their new grounds, for the inadequate Hyde Road enclosure had to be closed fully half-an-hour before the kick-off, and thousands of would-be spectators from Bolton and Manchester districts had to be refused admittance. As it was, the ground was overcrowded."*

United might have had a point and were simply

making a friendly gesture, but many associated with City considered the letter from Davies something of an insult, a money-making venture by United, more so as the Hyde Road club had splashed out around £5,000 in recent months on ground improvements, constructing a retaining wall and covering the stand and terraces on the popular side – something that Old Trafford could not boast. Neither was it the first time that United had attempted to entice their neighbours into using Old Trafford for a fixture, as they suggested that for the visit of the King to Hyde Road for the game against Liverpool the previous season that it might be more convenient to play the game across town.

The timing of United's offer could not have been more perfect, as Mangnall was to suddenly find even more work heaved upon his shoulders following a fire at Hyde Road on the night of Saturday November 6th 1920. Shortly before eleven o'clock, it was discovered that flames were coming from underneath the stand at the Hyde Road end of the ground. Although the fire brigade answered the call promptly, the fire had spread rapidly through the wooden construction and the stand and adjacent buildings were almost entirely enveloped in flames by the time they arrived. This included dressing rooms, offices, baths and attendants' rooms. A newspaper report added: *"In just over an hour the whole building, which was valued at several thousands of pounds, was razed to the ground. The flames could be seen for miles around and thousands of people were attracted to the ground. A strong body of police were drafted to the scene but great numbers of people by that time had flocked on to the other stands and made themselves comfortable to watch the rapid progress of the flames. It was an excited crowd, especially when the supports of the roof collapsed.*

The leaping flames revealed many hundreds of people sitting packed together as on the occasion of some big match. The stand was capable of seating about 8,000. people, and in view of the club's difficulties with regards to accommodation the loss is a very serious one. Nothing is known as to how the fire originated."

At first light the following day, Mangnall assembled a small army of men at the ground, clearing away the debris and preparing the ground for re-building to start. In all honesty, he hadn't had to look far for his temporary work-force, as fifty or sixty men, sensing work, turned up at the ground and were immediately employed. The *Manchester Evening News* reported that *"it might be an exaggeration to say that they were all City enthusiasts, but the fact remains that in the course of the morning, they effected such a transformation as would have staggered most contractors."*

Intent on getting the necessary work completed for the forthcoming match against Huddersfield Town three days later, Mangnall organised Well's lights to be set up so that work could continue after darkness had fallen in an attempt to get Hyde Road back to some form of normality. For that visit of Huddersfield Town on November 13th Mangnall also secured the use of a building from neighbours Galloway's for use as dressing rooms, while the actual attendance was recorded as around 30,000 which was in keeping with the current average.

A renewed offer for the use of Old Trafford had also been forthcoming, as the City directors had not yet replied to the original letter, but even with the fire, they decided that Hyde Road was their home and they would remain there, for the time being at least. As it was Mangnall and his motley crew of helpers, along with the skilled tradesmen managed to achieve the impossible in getting the ground up to scratch, whilst at the same time also managing to increase the ground capacity by 10,000, having a new stand in use for the visit of United on November 27th. Not only did they have a new stand, they had also somehow managed to incorporate dressing rooms and offices.

Having managed to regain some form of normality off the field, Mangnall strived to get his team into a favourable position in the First Division and between the fire and the end of January 1921 they were to lose only two games, leaving them fourth. Although they were seven points adrift of leaders Burnley, they were only one behind second and third-placed Newcastle United and Bolton Wanderers but things changed rapidly as only one win from four February fixtures knocked them back down to eighth and thirteen points adrift of leaders Burnley and seven behind second placed Newcastle.

It must have been disappointing for the City manager to see his side crumble, more so as he had now celebrated twenty-one years in football management and was to be presented with a long-service medal from the Football League. But it was another league championship medal he craved and if that was going to be achieved then the busy Easter programme, with double headers against leaders Burnley and Middlesbrough over the course of seven days was going to require maximum points from those four fixtures.

A 2-1 victory over Middlesbrough at Hyde Road on March 25th was an ideal start and twenty-four hours later league leaders Burnley arrived at the ground amid total chaos. Half an hour before kick-off the gates were locked with thousands outside and once again those outside were of the opinion that they would not be denied entry and stormed the gates, with others climbing over hoardings in an effort to gain admission. As the invaders surged into the ground, those already inside were pushed over the barriers and onto the pitch, but much to Mangnall and his director's relief, no-one suffered serious injury. Order was restored as police rushed to the ground, but hundreds still remained outside, many deciding to climb onto the roof of nearby cottages in order to catch a glimpse of the action.

Action there certainly was, as Hyde Road was again to suffer fire damage that afternoon, when a discarded cigarette caused a small fire in the temporary stand which was quickly put out with buckets of water – although it could quite easily have easily turned into something much more serious. On the pitch, City defeated the league leaders 3-0 and although they were still nine points adrift, they were only two behind second placed Liverpool and victories at Middlesbrough and Burnley in the days that followed would maintain that challenge.

Drifting back to the visit of Burnley and the scenes that prevailed prior to the ninety minutes, a few days following the fixture Mangnall, whilst sifting through the correspondence of the day, opened a letter with a postal order for one shilling enclosed. The letter read: *"Dear Sir. Enclosed please find P.O. for 1s., being my admission money for Saturday March 26. I had nothing to do with the break in, but the way was open, and I took it, and was delighted with a splendid exhibition."* At least one City supporter had a guilty conscience.

That supporter, however, was to see his favourite's championship challenge falter, as both those away fixtures against Burnley and Middlesbrough resulted in defeat, 3-1 in the north-east and 2-1 at Turf Moor, results that were to prove crucial in the weeks that followed. Seven fixtures remained, while Burnley had half a dozen, but suddenly, with each passing ninety minutes the championship dream drew closer and closer. Following their 2-1 victory over City, Burnley, for one reason or another hit the buffers, losing 2-0 at West Bromwich Albion and going on to draw 1-1 in the return fixture with the Albion and then recording a similar score line, home and away, against Everton. City in the meantime defeated Sheffield United 2-1 at Hyde Road, took a point from the 1-1 draw against the same side at Bramall Lane, then hit five past Preston North End in a 5-1 win at Hyde Road, before taking four points off Bradford Park Avenue in the home and away fixtures against the Yorkshire club.

Although those results were weighed in City's favour, the odd points that Burnley picked up from those drawn games, the victory over City, plus the points advantage they had built up earlier in the season, were enough for them to lift the First Division championship, Mangnall having to be content with second place, five points behind. Considering everything that City had gone through during the past ten months, it was an achievement to finish in such a prominent position.

Monday May 30th 1921 saw Ernest Mangnall presented with his long service medal by Football League president Mr. J. McKenna at the AGM of the League in the Connaught Rooms, London, a perfect fifty-seventh birthday present. It was certainly a notable achievement, but he craved for more, not from a personal point of view, but for Manchester City and football in general. If he felt that he could help a worthy cause then he was not slow in coming forward and being manager of Manchester City saw no barriers erected nor bias shown. This was never more obvious than in February 1922 when he was appointed a trustee of the John Robson Memorial Fund.

Robson had been manager of Manchester United but stepped down through ill-health in October 1921 and had passed away following a short illness on January 11th leaving a widow and young children. A benefit match was arranged and was different from others as it was also a Football League trial match in order to pick a team to face the Scottish League in Glasgow in March. Played at Old Trafford, the game raised £1,237 2s 10d, with the League giving all the proceeds to the fund, while donations produced a further £756 17s 11d. United donated one hundred guineas to the fund. If there was one thing that Mangnall could master, then it was the handling of money and he was noted as being a shrewd operator, as twenty-one of the twenty-eight players that he had at his disposal for the 1922-23 season had not cost a penny. But he was certainly no Scrooge, as if money had to be paid out for the benefit of an organisation or a club, then he would certainly sanction it. Neither could he ever be accused as being 'work-shy', as not only did the summer of 1922 see him busy in preparation for the coming season, he had at long last seen Manchester City make plans to move away from the cramped surroundings of Hyde Road.

Belle Vue had, for some considerable time, been considered as an ideal location for City's new ground but this was a move that Mangnall strongly opposed and he finally managed to use his persuasive powers in May 1922 when it was announced that the club had purchased just over sixteen acres of land near Whitworth Park for £3,500. Initial accommodation was given as 15,000 seated and 65,000 under cover, but it was mentioned that there was enough room to expand and accommodate 100,000, making it what Mangnall and his directors could claim – 'The Wembley of the North'. Perhaps it was of no mere coincidence that the construction contract was given to Sir Robert McAlpine and Co., who were at that time also involved in the construction of the Empire Stadium at Wembley. Work was planned to commence on the new ground in June 1922 and it was planned to be operational for the start of the 1923-24 season.

1921-22 saw City finish 10th in the First Division and a look at the results could well be nothing more than a mirror image of previous campaigns. The three defeats that bridged November and December, ending with a 5-0 hammering at Bolton, more or less put paid to any title hopes. Three games without a win in February and the forward line drawing blanks in four games during March, showed that they were some distance away from title contention.

Season 1922-23 was little better, although City did finish a couple of places higher, but once again, it was that old failing – in fifteen of the forty-two fixtures City's attack drew a blank! Saturday April 28th was one of those occasions, a goalless draw against Newcastle United but it was a game that did not simply bring down the curtain on the home fixtures for that season, but saw league football played at Hyde Road for the last time, before just 18,000 supporters. 'Icarus' of the *Athletic News* describing it as a "drab finale". By this stage critics were accusing Mangnall of paying more attention to off-field matters than those on the pitch. Perhaps they were right, but much depended on the move and, as with United's stadium switch, it was difficult to dampen Mangnall's enthusiasm.

Hyde Road might have been a thing of the past, but with the season over there was still much to be done and Mangnall's name was seldom out of the papers – "TO FOOTBALL CLUBS, CRICKET CLUBS ~ Manchester City Football Club are open to receive offers for the whole of the Covered Stand (steel) and large open Woodwork Stand. &c., on the ground at Hyde Road. Open inspection every week-day. - J. MANGNALL. Secretary." – "TENDERS. MANCHESTER CITY F.C. INVITE TENDERS for Sole Rights of PRINTING and SELLING OFFICIAL PROGRAMMES, CATERING (Refreshments, &c.), SALE OF CHOCOLATES, SWEETS, ICE CREAM, &c., on the New Ground, Maine Road, Moss Side. during season. 1923-1924. J. E. MANGNALL, Secretary."

The City secretary also had a constant trickle of visitors knocking on his office door wanting a sneak preview of the new ground. One group of individuals were not football minded, but consisted of the Honorary Secretary of the Scottish Rugby Union and some members of the Executive Committee. The Scottish Union were about to lay out a new ground at Murrayfield, Edinburgh, and thought that they would like see the latest creation of this kind, as the ground was considered both *"spacious and thoughtfully laid out, with turf that was fit for a match at either cricket or bowls."*

By the time of the opening First Division fixture against Sheffield United on August 25th, City had moved, lock stock and barrel. On the eve of the new season, the *Manchester Evening News* contained the following:

> *"That this vast stadium should have been practically completed between April 24 and August 24 of this year is the subject for wonder and admiration. It unquestionably creates a record in building construction, and it is a splendid testimonial to*

the organising powers of the contractors, Sir Robert McAlpine and Sons.

"Most people were freely sceptical as to whether the enclosure would be ready for tomorrow. A month ago, it did not seem possible that it could be, but by the employment of hundreds of skilled workmen all but the internal work on the huge stand has been completed, and even this remaining task will not occupy more than a fortnight."

Twenty-four hours later the same paper could barely master its enthusiasm:

"A GREAT MULTITUDE - City's New Ground a Great Attraction - STIRRING SCENES - Moss Side Thrown Off Its Balance." Not one headline, but four! It continued: "The great trek to the new Manchester City ground began in almost sensational fashion. Shortly after one o'clock a huge throng of people began to disgorge itself on the main Wilmslow Road, and from that time, for at least an hour afterwards, the volume of traffic, vehicular and pedestrian, was such as this fine highway has never seen before.

"The people of Rusholme and Greenheys rose to the occasion mightily. On all the numerous inlets to the ground there were people assembled at street corners merely to see the crowds pass, as though it was to these residents a spectacle of an extraordinary character. Near to the ground enterprising people had already got busy in all manner of ways of making a shilling or two out of the occasion. There were mendicants and hawkers innumerable; the boys selling the City programmes

had spread themselves far afield and there were
booths and stalls, tables and boxes, on which were
displayed alluring sweets and confections, pies and
black puddings, and other toothsome comestibles
likely to tickle the palate of the surging mob.

"ENTHUSIASTIC PEDESTRIANS. It
was noticeable long before the kick-off that very
many of the thousands who were wending their
way to the ground had decided to foot it through
the maze of streets leading to what was probably
to them an unfamiliar district. In this way very
many thousands came from the direction of Hulme,
Chorlton-on-Medlock, Longsight, Ardwick,
Levenshulme, Fallowfield, Chorlton-cum-Hardy
and even districts a greater distance away.

"It was quite obvious that the new and strange
rendezvous had puzzled the crowd as to the best
means of approach, and despite the very elaborate
provisions made by the Manchester Tramway
department, and the directions given concerning
the use of the new and extended services. Cars
were not anything like as prominent in bringing
the multitude to the ground at the outset. Later
on, however, the cars were getting their full due of
passengers, and more, and the various routes were
splendidly patronised.

"AN HOUR BEFORE THE START.
There was plenty of evidence long before two o'clock
that the crowd was going to be an immense one.
Even at that hour the huge stands on the popular
side were thickly lined with eager enthusiasts, many
of whom wore the City colours. It was noticeable,
too, that, these hardy robust supporters had rigged

themselves out for the occasion almost to a man with new and light-coloured caps.

"It was a brave and stirring scene as the multitude gradually filled the ground and the stream of traffic, both on foot and wheel, seemed to be unending. So far from being disturbed or nonplussed by the unusual experience of a journey into Rusholme the city stalwarts seemed to enjoy the novelty of it, exceedingly, and they were in a high state of revelry long before the actual proceeding of the day began.

"CLAMOUR HEARD FOR MILES AROUND. The assembling of so vast a throng quite threw the good people of Moss Side and Rusholme off their balance. There was a new note of tumultuous excitement in the air, and it penetrated to every corner of the district, its clamour being heard for many miles around. Even the birds seemed to be participating in a rare occasion, for they were flocking about the ground in excited flocks, and could not settle down to the rich feed of luscious green grass of the playing space which attracted them to the enclosure. The gate was, indeed, a tremendous one, and half an hour before play commenced it seemed impossible that the huge concourse of people still arriving could find accommodation, at any rate on the popular stands.

"A very large force of police kept admirable order under conditions which must have tried them exceedingly. The crowd enjoyed itself hugely during the time of waiting. They accompanied with great gusto the popular tunes played by the Beswick Old Prize Band, and a number of them clambered over *the palisading and executed foxtrots and the wild whirling of Indian and Egyptian ballet dancing, to the vast amusement of the thousands of onlookers.*

"DISPLAY OF COLOURS. - There was a profuse display of the City colours, carried out in various forms. A few wild spirits were arrayed in the familiar blue and white, and others carried umbrellas or streamers of the same colouring. There was but a few minutes to wait for the kick-off but the immense throng was still being added to in seemingly unending streams. The banked crowd on the popular side, ranging tier upon tier double the height of the neighbouring housetops, presented at magnificent and impressive spectacle of moving, pulsating, and excited humanity."

Unlike that final game at Hyde Road, Maine Road was christened in a blaze of glory with a 2-1 victory after the ground had been officially opened by the Lord Mayor and no major hitch was recorded, with the *Athletic News* reporting:

"Manchester City have scored a decided success, for the ground has been designed after much thought by Mr. C. Swain, who at a dinner on Saturday night to celebrate the occasion, acknowledged his great indebtedness to J. E. Mangnall, the City secretary, who had so carefully advised him in reference to the many details that materially contribute to the clear view, convenience, and comfort of the spectators. Mr. Swain, the architect, in replying to toast, stated that was engaged three years ago to design new ground for Manchester City. Since that time, he had passed through many sleepless nights. At first it was

*suggested that the site should be at Belle Vue, but
there were only eight acres of land available, and
that would only give accommodation for 30,000 or
40,000 people. Manchester City declared that that
was of no use, and they decided to go Moss Side,
and there he had been able to lay out an enclosure
capable of taking 90,000 people with a seating
capacity for 10,000 on the grandstand."*

56,993 were present for that opening fixture, but strangely,
the Saturday afternoons that followed failed to induce
similar sized crowds, nor did they keep Mangnall overly
busy counting the silver and copper coins, as a couple of
forty-odd thousand crowds were the next best they were
to manage amid indifferent results.

Having been a formidable influence behind United's
Old Trafford, Mangnall now had another feather in his cap
with the construction of Maine Road, but he still craved
silverware. One victory from the opening half dozen
fixture of 1923-24 did not bode well for the campaign
ahead, with inconsistency and a dozen draws throughout
the season doing little to promote thoughts of the First
Division title arriving any day soon but the F.A. Cup and
its one-off ninety minute encounters was a completely
different scenario altogether. Nottingham Forest were the
visitors at Maine Road for the F. A. Cup first round tie
on January 12th and goals from Roberts and Barnes in a
2-1 win saw those first steps towards the final taken, but
that journey almost came to an abrupt end in round two
when they found themselves 2-1 down to Halifax Town
before a late equaliser forced a replay. Halifax performed
equally well, perhaps even more so, in the replay on their
home soil and even with an additional half an hour, the

score line continued goalless. So, it was on to a third game at Old Trafford, where City finally managed to overcome the Yorkshire side with a convincing 3-0 victory.

City made no doubt of the result in round three as Brighton were hammered 5-1 on the south coast, but round four was once again not for the faint hearted as Cardiff City left Manchester to live for another day on the back of a 0-0 draw. Four days later, a Browell goal was all that separated the sides and edged Manchester City into the semi-finals. They may have been just one step from Wembley but the ninety minutes against Newcastle United did not live up to expectations. Many had City down as favourites, but on the day they were beaten by a far superior team, losing 2-0, with the north-east side going on to lift the cup in the second Wembley final with a 2-0 win over Aston Villa.

Mangnall took the defeat hard, harder perhaps than many realised, as a matter of days later he announced that he was stepping down. "Manchester City Secretary to Resign" – *Sheffield Daily Telegraph* Monday April 7th – "*Surprise will be created in football circles by the news that Mr. J. E. Mangnall is to sever his connection with Manchester City Club, of which he has been secretary since 1912. It is alleged that there has been internal friction, and the directors have decided not to renew his agreement, which terminates at the end of this season.*"

The *Athletic News* of the same day carried the following:

> "*Dropping the Pilot. The Manchester City Football Club and Mr. Ernest Mangnall, the secretary, are about to part company. The severance of this association seems to us matter for regret and cause of deep anxiety. No man has accomplished*

more for the elevation of Manchester football. A native of Bolton, Ernest Mangnall was educated at the local grammar school, and after playing his part as a boy and an adult in football, athletics, cycling, and swimming with considerable success in 1900 took the thankless office of secretary to Burnley. In October, 1903, was elected similar post in connection with Manchester United, and was associated with their rebuilding and historic triumphs in The League and the Association Cup. During the summer of 1912 he crossed the road, so to speak, and accepted the same position with Manchester City. Next month his agreement runs out and is not to be renewed. Both the United and the City clubs benefited by his experience and forethought.

"Each club in turn has had fine teams, and each has during his tenure of office obtained and equipped new grounds which are features of the city. It would be absurd to think that such stupendous changes could have been carried out without the co-operation of the far-seeing secretary. When Mr. Mangnall was appointed to take charge of the affairs of Manchester City we said that the directors of that club had chosen well, and we hoped that the City, which had been overwhelmed with trouble, would benefit by his experience, his qualifications, and ripe judgment, and would retain the confidence of the Board.

"This he has done for nearly twelve years, during which he has proved himself a fine organiser, shrewd financier, and man of character. His work would stand the closest investigation, and it does *seem strange to drop the pilot just when the club has embarked upon an enterprise such as the Maine-road [sic] ground and his particular qualities as a manager are most needed.*

"Into domestic reasons which have caused the severance of the co-partnership between the board and their secretary we cannot enter. It is not our business; it is a matter for inquiry by the shareholders. But we should have thought that the directorate would have striven to bridge any gulf, to overcome any misunderstanding or difficulty before depriving the club, at such a time as this, of the help of such thoroughly practical and thoughtful man who has shown originality in a constructive sense and minute care in working out details. The club has lost its head and right arm, and it will be indeed difficult to replace him."

The curtain came down on Mangnall's Mancunian football career on Saturday May 3rd 1924 when West Ham United travelled north to Maine Road for the final fixture of the season. It would have been more fitting had it been another United in opposition, but the red shirted version from a short distance across town were by then a Second Division side.

"Manchester's Tribute to Mr. J. E. Mangnall" was the heading on an article in the *Athletic News* on Monday May 5th, which went on to say:

"Mr. J. E. Mangnall terminates his agreement with Manchester City at the end of this month, and the esteem in which he has been held both by the players and supporters of the club was attested at the conclusion of the match with West Ham United

at Moss Side on Saturday. The players presented
him with a gold watch, and the members of the
Ground Committee with a silver cigar case and
match-box.

"M. Hamill, handing over the players', token,
spoke of Mr. Mangnall as a "boss and a pal," to
whom no player had gone with a grievance in which
he had not elicited satisfaction, and J. F. Mitchell,
the amateur international goalkeeper, who presided
at the ceremony, said they had always regarded him
as the "players' friend."

"The Ground Committee, through their
chairman, regretted the severance and recalled
with pardonable pride the good relationship which
had always existed between Mr. Mangnall and
themselves."

The gold watch presented to the departing secretary
contained his monogram and the words "Presented to J.
E. Mangnall by the players of Manchester City F. C. to
mark the respect and esteem they had for him during his
term of office as secretary and manager 1912-1924."

Although the curtain had fallen on his career, there
was, like many a big-name act, an encore. This was not
simply a walk out onto the Maine Road pitch, a wave to
the support and then a seat in the director's box to watch
some nondescript ninety minutes. No, J. E. Mangnall
deserved much more than that and he got it in the form
of a testimonial match on September 10th 1924, when
a combined Manchester XI faced a Merseyside XI at
Maine Road.

There were many memories of Mangnall the football
man, like the one that appeared in the *Sheffield Green 'Un*,
under the heading – "A Mangnall Memory" and written

by J. T. Howcroft a famous Cup Final referee. It read:

> *"The arrangement of a testimonial match to Mr. J. E. Mangnall, the late secretary and manager of the Manchester City club, reminds me of his earlier years. It is many a long day since I first met him, and it may not be generally known that he was one if not the first of Bolton men to ride a penny-farthing - one of the high bicycles used in old days - from Land's End to John o' Groats. Travelling with Bolton Wanderers to London to play a friendly game with the 'Spurs, many years ago, when Mr. Mangnall was a director of the Bolton club, I was invited to officiate as linesman. Unfortunately, I had no boots, but the 'Spurs' trainer fixed me up with a pair of nines. Now as I only take sevens, I had considerable difficulty in moving about freely, and even the referee took umbrage and would not take the slightest notice of my decisions, much to the disgust of Mr Mangnall. The latter came along to me at half time and said: "Hand me those boots. They will fit me better than you, and I will make the referee take notice of me." He did!*

For some unknown reason, the testimonial match did not attract the attention of the Manchester footballing public as a mere 10,000 turned up, with the Liverpool XI running out winners by the odd goal in five. Following the fixture, the Manchester United programme editor included the following in his match programme against Coventry City:

> *"The match between the combined Manchester and Liverpool sides at Maine-road [sic] on Wednesday must be voted a success, comparatively, at all events.*

*The result does not matter, but we should liked
to have seen a much bigger crowd present. Ernest
Mangnall has done splendid service for football
generally and Manchester in particular, and in
a city of its population one would have thought
there would have been at least 20,000 sufficiently
supportive of it to attend. The football public have
notoriously short memories. The more's the pity."*

Despite the poor attendance, it was estimated that
around £500 was raised.

Having given up his day job, one that certainly never kept
regular hours, Mangnall remained in football, retaining
his interest in the League Managers and Secretary's
Association and also the Central League, both of which
he founded, with the latter now considered one of the
best run in the game. Although his name came up now
and again when a managerial vacancy arose, he was never
tempted back behind a desk on a daily basis.

Following his Maine Road departure, City soon found
themselves heading to the Second Division at the end of
the 1925-26 season, but were to spring back as champions
at the end of the 1927-28 campaign. His legacy lived on
much better at Moss Side than at Old Trafford, but it was
not enough to see him granted admission to Maine Road
for City's match against Bury in February 1926.

On a previous occasion, on what had been his first
visit to the ground since his departure, he overheard a
City director saying to the commissionaire on the main
entrance – "Don't let him in unless he has a ticket."
Producing his Lancashire Football Association pass, he was
allowed admission. But when he tried to gain admission
to the Bury match he was stopped in his tracks, with the

commissionaire saying that he had instructions not to let him in. Knocked back by the rejection, he sought out a Mr. Duckworth, a Bury director, explained his plight and was given a visiting director's ticket allowing him admission. It was a poor show from a club for whom he had done so much.

For all his endeavours in the world of football, Ernest Mangnall should have been blessed with a long and happy retirement, enjoying the fresh sea breezes blowing along the front at Lytham St Annes. Unfortunately, this was not to be, as the *Athletic News* of April 30th 1928 reported that he had been suffering lately from a very serious illness. He was still reported as being unwell two months later, but made something of a recovery, maintaining his eagle-eyed interest in the affairs of the game as a member of the Lancashire Football Association until May 1931.

Eight months later, on Thursday January 14th 1932, James Ernest Mangnall passed away at his home, 3 Osborne Road, Lytham St Annes. His death was lamented far and wide and his funeral saw large numbers gather to pay their respects as he was laid to rest in Lytham Cemetery.

In his will, Ernest Mangnall left the sum of £9,497, but he left much more than that to Manchester and English football, things that no amount of money could ever buy.

But as we draw to an end the story of a remarkable man, let us drift back to Manchester United. The club's history is vast and varied and if you were to ask most supporters to name the club's most important manager it would be a toss-up between Sir Matt Busby and Sir Alex Ferguson as to who would get the most votes. James Ernest Mangnall would most probably not receive a mention, but it was this Lancastrian who brought the

First Division championship to the club for the first time, followed soon afterwards by the club's inaugural F.A. Cup, trophies that both Busby and Ferguson were also to win many years later, but what is forgotten is the fact that it was James Ernest Mangnall who set the United mould.

11: A Lasting Tribute

I MENTIONED IN THE INTRODUCTION how my interest in James Ernest Mangnall came about through my work with the Manchester United Graves Society. Having located his grave in Lytham Cemetery, a friend who happened to be in the area paid a visit and sent me the photographs he had taken of the grave. In his email, he wrote:

> "By pure chance I needed to be in Lytham today so I popped along to the cemetery. Tricky to find the actual grave but here are the pics [see introduction]. No obvious outward sign that it is his grave. You will see that the cross has been laid down, but I recognised his daughter's name on the side of the lower plinth. I think the cemetery people have laid lots of monuments down over time for safety reasons. His date of death and his wife's details are on the face of the lower plinth.
>
> "I had to raise the cross upright so that his name (which had been on the underneath side of the fallen cross) was visible. It is on the face of the upper plinth (as was). The last pic shows his name. This grave looks like a very good candidate for refurbishment and possible enhancement."

Without Phil's final comment, I was of the opinion that this had the making of a project and one that I again mentioned in the introduction to this book. I contacted another friend, a Manchester based, and United supporting, stonemason, who had worked on refurbishing Harold Hardman's grave and had also worked on Sir Matt Busby's, told him what was required, sending him the photos, and asked him for a price. This was forthcoming, and eventually, through no fault whatsoever of Paul the stonemason, the work was carried out and as you can see from the 'before and after' shots, the work carried out by McGarry Memorials of Manchester on September 9th 2019, was excellent and worthy of the man it commemorates.

Without the Manchester United Graves Society the final resting place of Ernest Mangnall would have remained in a sorry state, uncared for, as it had been for many years. Too long. His is not the only grave to be like this and through the interest by supporters in the 'Society' others have seen a tidy up, but not on the same scale as Mangnall's. Too many, unfortunately, lie in unmarked graves, but hopefully in the future, the 'Society' can get more work carried out in a way of saying thanks to those who played a part in the history of Newton Heath and Manchester United.

If you are ever anywhere near Lytham St Annes, pop over to the cemetery and pay your respects to James Ernest Mangnall, the man who made the United mould.

The grave can be found at Lytham Park Cemetery – A – 512 C/E. When you go through the gates, take the path to your right. It is on the left as you walk up.

INDEX